REMNANT REVIVAL

30 Days to Awakening the Disciple Within

A. Alvez, J.D.

Scripture quotations are taken from the following Bible translations:

- Scripture quotations marked *NLT* are taken from the *Holy Bible, New Living Translation*, copyright © 1996, 2004, 2015 by Tyndale House Foundation. Used by permission of Tyndale House Publishers, Carol Stream, Illinois 60188. All rights reserved.

- Scripture quotations marked *ESV* are from *The Holy Bible, English Standard Version®, ESV®*, copyright © 2001 by Crossway, a publishing ministry of Good News Publishers. Used by permission. All rights reserved.

- Scripture quotations marked *ICB* are from the *International Children's Bible®, ICB®*, copyright © 1986, 1988, 1999, 2015 by Tommy Nelson. Used by permission. All rights reserved.

- Scripture quotations marked *NASB2020* are from the *New American Standard Bible®*, Copyright © 2020 by The Lockman Foundation. Used by permission. All rights reserved.

- Scripture quotations marked *TPT* are from *The Passion Translation®*. Copyright © 2017, 2018, 2020 by Brian Simmons and BroadStreet Publishing® Group, LLC. Used by permission. All rights reserved. The Passion Translation® is a registered trademark of BroadStreet Publishing® Group, LLC.

- Scripture quotations marked *MSG* are taken from *The Message*. Copyright © 1993, 1994, 1995, 1996, 2000, 2001, 2002 by Eugene H. Peterson. Used by permission of NavPress. All rights reserved. Represented by Tyndale House Publishers, Inc.

Cover and interior design by Valeria Alvez
Printed in the United States of America
First Edition
ISBN: 979-8-218-71507-6

Acknowledgments

First and foremost, all glory, honor, and praise belong to God. This book would not exist without the leading of the Holy Spirit, whose presence stirred a holy urgency within me to call the Church—His bride—back to awakening. Thank You, Father, for entrusting me with this assignment. May every word point back to You.

To the remnant—those still hungry, still burning, still listening—this is for you. May your fire never go out.

To my husband, Alexis—thank you for being the constant covering for our family in prayer, standing beside me in faith even when the details of God's assignments are unclear. You trust what He's doing in me, even when you don't see the full picture, and that trust strengthens me more than you know. Your love is steady, your support is sacrificial, and your prayers are powerful. You often remind me that you fell in love with me because I'm unique—and when the calling feels heavy or misunderstood, those words remind me that God designed me this way on purpose. Thank you for seeing that and loving me through it all.

To my daughter, Valeria—your prayers carry us more than you know. I know it's because of your intercession that God activates projects like these in our lives. Thank you for your faith, your joy, and for using your gifts to illustrate this book so beautifully. Your heart for God inspires me daily. You are a humble leader with a heart for God's mission—we know God is going to use you powerfully for His Kingdom.

To my Pastors, Mark and Ann Pecina, at Faith Builders Worship Center—thank you for the passion and spiritual fire you've demonstrated through the years. I pray this book blesses you as deeply as your ministry has blessed us.

To my family and my church—you inspired these pages. I wrote this with you in mind and heart, and I truly hope you'll read every word. My greatest desire is that you learn from it, grow through it, and encounter Jesus afresh through these truths.

To those who have warred for me in prayer, encouraged me in weakness, and believed in the message when it was still forming— thank you. You are part of this revival.

May this book awaken a generation. May it stir dry bones. And may it always glorify the One who is worthy of it all—Jesus Christ.

Prayerfully,
Amanda

Awakening the Remnant:
The Call to Rise

This book wasn't written out of convenience—it was written out of conviction.

There is an urgency in the Spirit. A call to wake up. A call to rise. A call to return to the power, purity, and purpose of real discipleship. Many in the Church have fallen asleep with their eyes wide open—going through motions, checking the boxes, but lacking fire. And it's costing us dearly.

We see it everywhere:
Faith reduced to performance.
Church attendance without transformation.
Believers trained to consume, but not to carry the cross.

And after COVID-19? The shaking was undeniable. But instead of awakening, many settled. The Church came back—but not all came back burning. Reverence was replaced with routine. Hunger faded into habit. We forgot how to recognize the presence of God... and worse, many stopped looking altogether.

But God is still moving. And He's still calling.

Remnant Revival is for those who are done playing church. For the ones who can feel that the clock is ticking, and the world is shifting—and know that lukewarm faith won't carry us through what's coming. It's for the generation that refuses to sleep through their calling. For the hungry. For the ready. For the remnant.

If you've felt dry, distant, or disillusioned—don't settle.

There *is* more.

There *has to be* more.

And now is the time to go after it.

You haven't missed your moment.

You were born for this one.

So rise up.

Return.

Awaken the disciple within.

Because the Church doesn't need another program.

It needs you—fully alive.

This is more than a book—it's a 30-day discipleship journey designed to reignite your walk with Christ. Each day includes powerful scripture, reflective questions, and a focused prayer to anchor you in truth. In addition to the daily journey, you'll find a weekly discipleship group guide with discussion questions and prayer points to help you grow in community and accountability. This isn't just reading—it's revival.

"For a remnant of my people will spread out from Jerusalem, a group of survivors from Mount Zion. The passionate commitment of the Lord of Heaven's Armies will make this happen!"
2 Kings 19:31 NLT

Day 1:
Love

John 3:16 NLT
"For this is how God loved the world: He gave his one and only Son, so that everyone who believes in Him will not perish but have eternal life."

Somehow you accepted Jesus Christ as your Savior and believe that God sent His Son, the Messiah, Jesus Christ to die on the cross for your sins to be forgiven. Congratulations! You have met the One who can change everything. You feel different—you know there is a love there, and you feel it. But you don't quite understand what it all means. How do we become a disciple?

It starts with love—true love. There are preconceived notions we bring into every sphere of our lives, our stories shape us. However, the Kingdom of God is upside down. The Kingdom of God goes against everything the world around us accepts as true—beginning with love.

John 3:16 is the cornerstone of discipleship. This scripture encompasses the foundation of truth: love. This great God made you in His image, with a purpose that only you can fulfill. And though there is nothing you can do that even comes close to His goodness, righteousness, and perfection, He made a way for you to spend eternity with Him, in a place where there are no tears, no pain, and where peace and joy surpass all understanding.

God sent His only Son to die for you. Yahweh, the Messiah, came to earth, became flesh, and was persecuted, beaten, and hung on a cross to die for your sin. Jesus was sinless—the perfect man—the least deserving of death. But He chose to fully do the will of God and gave His life for you, to forgive you for the sins that Jesus (God in the flesh) would never commit. Can you imagine Jesus sitting with you while you commit sin? Yet Jesus was nailed to the cross for that sin.

And because God loves you so much, if you believe that Jesus came to die for your sin, Jesus will be your righteousness at the time of judgment—taking the punishment for your sin and saving you. Jesus teaches us a critical part of discipleship: love is the ultimate sacrifice—denying yourself completely for the will of God and reconciliation.

Discipleship

Scriptures: John 3:16
Additional Scriptures: John 15:13

Questions:

1. What does true love mean to you? Write down a few words or phrases that come to mind when you think about true love.

2. Jesus Christ demonstrated true love by laying down His life for you (John 15:13). There is no greater love than that. How is this different from the kind of love you've experienced in your own life?

3. In your own words, what does it mean to *deny yourself* as a disciple of Christ?

Prayer: *Thank you, God, for sending Your One and Only Son, Jesus Christ, to die for me. I have never experienced a love like Yours and I am so grateful for Your love and sacrifice. Please open my mind, heart, and eyes to who You are and help me to walk in Your righteousness. I come to you, Father God, humbly asking for Your forgiveness for all the times I have fallen into sin. I thank You, Jesus my Savior, for giving Your life for me. In Your name, Jesus, Amen.*

Day 2:
Faith

John 3:16 NLT
"For this is how God loved the world: He gave his one and only Son, so that everyone who believes in Him will not perish but have eternal life."

I know what you're thinking—this was yesterday's verse. But there is more to unpack, just stay with me. The summation of the gospel is found in John 3:16 and Ephesians 2:8-9.

"God saved you by his grace when you believed. And you can't take credit for this; it is a gift from God. Salvation is not a reward for the good things we have done, so none of us can boast about it."
Ephesians 2:8-9 NLT

So how do we reconcile the message of John 3:16 and Ephesians 2:8-9 with the passage in Matthew 7:13-14?

"You can enter God's Kingdom only through the narrow gate. The highway to hell is broad, and its gate is wide for the many who choose that way. But the gateway to life is very narrow and the road is

difficult, and only a few ever find it. "
Matthew 7:13-14 NLT

If the key to salvation is the gospel—salvation through the death and resurrection of Jesus Christ for us—then what connects our belief in Jesus to finding the narrow gate that leads to life?

It's our faith.

The scripture in John and in Ephesians emphasizes that we must believe – it is required. But what does true belief look like?

Every day we get up and go to work, knowing that eventually we will be paid for that work. Every day we get up, we grab the keys to our car, go open the door, sit in the car, put the key in the ignition, all the while knowing that when we turn the key, the car is going to start. **There is a *knowing*.** Rarely do we doubt any of these things are going to happen. In fact, if we did not believe we would get paid for our job, we probably wouldn't show up.

Do we sometimes not show up with God?

Over this first week, we will explore what faith truly looks like in the life of a disciple.

Discipleship

Scriptures: John 3:16, Ephesians 2:8-9, Matthew 7:13-14
Additional Scriptures: Hebrews 11:3, Mark 11:22

Questions:

1. What do you think the "highway to hell" looks like?

2. What does the narrow road to life look like?

3. What do you really believe in? List some examples from your daily life—things you know will happen, no matter what.

Prayer: *Lord God, please reveal to me the things in my life that lead me down the broad road to hell. Please help me to recognize the things that exalt You, my God and Your Kingdom and help me to see the narrow road that I need to walk to glorify only You. Help me with my unbelief, God. In the marvelous name of Jesus, Amen.*

Day 3:
Little Faith

Matthew 17:15-20 ESV

"'Lord, have mercy on my son, for he has seizures and he suffers terribly. For often he falls into the fire, and often into the water. And I brought him to your disciples, and they could not heal him.' And Jesus answered, 'O faithless and twisted generation, how long am I to be with you? How long am I to bear with you? Bring him here to me.' And Jesus rebuked the demon, and it came out of him, and the boy was healed instantly. Then the disciples came to Jesus privately and said, 'Why could we not cast it out?' He said to them, 'Because of your little faith. For truly, I say to you, if you have faith like a grain of mustard seed, you will say to this mountain, 'Move from here to there,' and it will move, and nothing will be impossible for you.'"

Over the next three days we will discuss the **three roots of doubt** that grow within our faith. We will learn to recognize these roots and begin to refine our faith by pruning out doubt.

The first root of doubt is **little faith**. Like the disciples in Matthew 17, we may struggle with having little faith. The power of faith that God has given us allows us to tell the mountain to move, and it shall move—nothing shall be impossible for us. That sounds amazing!

However, I will be the first to admit—having that type of faith is difficult when the unpaid bills are piling up and are too far behind, or the doctor is giving a life-altering diagnosis, or a loved one dies far too young. But that's me in the flesh, not the real me who is called by God. God, in His lovingkindness, understands the difficulty of faith in the darkest moments. That is why He gave us His Word. Scripture equips us with the tools to identify and uproot the roots of our doubt.

So, what do we do when we suffer with little faith? We apply Mark 9:23-24.

"And Jesus said to him, 'If you can'! All things are possible for one who believes.' Immediately the father of the child cried out and said, 'I believe; help my unbelief!'"
Mark 9:23-24 ESV

There is profound revelation in this passage. We realize that it is not about applying a biblical standard, don't misunderstand me – that is the end result – but it's the end result because the Word of God teaches us the outcome of a *relationship* with the One who loves us, our Savior Jesus Christ.

You see, even when the father didn't have it completely right – saying, "I believe," and then asking Jesus to help him with his unbelief – Jesus still cast out the demon from his child. **The revelation is in the response**. When you are in the depths of darkness, how do you respond? Or more importantly—*to whom* do you respond?

Notice: the father didn't fake it. He didn't stand in front of Jesus, after Jesus said anything is possible for those who believe, and say I believe. He confessed his struggle with unbelief—and Jesus honored the father's sincerity.

This passage sparked a deep discussion in my home about how we pray in those moments where our belief is shaky—when we are not truly 100% believing, in faith, something will happen. Many times, we put the burden of faith back on God, we try to make our prayers sound spiritual, like, "Please God, if this is your will then let it happen." But what if the father in Mark 9 had said, "I believe—if it's Your will?" Would Jesus have responded the same?

Of course, it is the will of God that a child be freed from demonic oppression.

If we are praying from a place where we are unsure if our request is the will of God, then we cannot pray from a place of faith. Instead, we need to pray for direction, instruction, and the will of God to be revealed.

"You can pray for anything and if you have faith, you will receive it." Matthew 21:22 NLT

When we pray for something that we know is the will of God, we can pray boldly and with the faith God requires of us. We must ask God to help our unbelief when His will requires an increase in our faith.

Discipleship

Scriptures: Matthew 17:15-20, Mark 9:23-24, Matthew 21:22
Additional Scriptures: Hebrews 11

Questions:

1. In what areas of your life do you struggle with little faith?

2. To respond correctly in difficult circumstances, we must recognize both how and to whom we respond when our faith is shaken. Who—or what—do you turn to in your hardest moments? *Example: When you are depressed, do you turn to drinking alcohol? When you are angry, do you respond by gossiping with a certain person?*

3. Create a plan that you can follow to replace the bad responses with turning to Jesus. What would that look like in practical terms?

Prayer: *Thank you, God, for helping me with my unbelief. Please help me to remember when I respond to the hard circumstances in the wrong way. Help me to break the bad responses and remove them from my life. Thank You for helping me build my faith, I want to glorify You in all things. In the precious name of Jesus, Amen.*

Day 4:
Our Will

The second root of doubt is **our will**.

"And this is the confidence that we have toward Him, that if we ask anything according to His will He hears us."
1 John 5:14 ESV

God's Word promises that when we ask for something according to His will, He hears us. 1 John 5:15 NLT continues saying that if God hears us then, *"...we also know that He will give us what we ask for."*

The promise, then, is this: **when we pray according to His will, He will hear us, and He will answer us – favorably.**

We cannot be discouraged when what we ask for does not come to pass the way we expected. It may not align with God's will. The greatness of who God is and what He sees is far beyond what we can understand in the moment. He reminds us of this in Isaiah:

"My thoughts are nothing like your thoughts,' says the Lord. 'And my ways are far beyond anything you could imagine."'
Isaiah 55:8 NLT

As we walk this narrow road, our wants, our needs, and desires will begin to align with the will of God. That alignment does not happen instantly—it is a process that happens when He prunes and refines us through His love. There are times throughout this process where we may be unsure of what the will of God is, instead of praying from a place of doubt, we can pray for His will to be made known.

Pray that God will give you complete knowledge of His will, as Paul and Timothy prayed for the people in the city of Colossae:

"So we have not stopped praying for you since we first heard about you. We ask God to give you complete knowledge of His will and to give you spiritual wisdom and understanding."
Colossians 1:9 NLT

The entirety of our faith is based on our belief—that's why it's called our faith. As we begin to use the tools our Father has given us to walk by faith, we will come to realize that there is never a moment where we have to question the goodness of God in our lives.

"And we know that God causes everything to work together for the good of those who love God and are called according to his purpose for them." Romans 8:28 NLT

His promise is that **He works everything for our good**. Though we may not see it, we are called to trust beyond what our flesh sees.

"So we don't look at the troubles we can see now; rather, we fix our gaze on things that cannot be seen. For the things we see now will soon be gone, but the things we cannot see will last forever." 2 Corinthians 4:18 NLT

We pray in faith when we ask God for something. But when we are uncertain if something is His will, we shift our prayer asking for His will to be made known to us.

Discipleship

Scriptures: 1 John 5:14, Isaiah 55:8, Colossians 1:9,
Romans 8:28, 2 Corinthians 4:18
Additional Scriptures: 1 Thessalonians 5:18, John 7:17

Questions:

1. What is the will of God for your life—or for a specific
situation in your life right now?

2. What are some desires, wants, or needs that you
recognize need to change in order to align with God's will?

3. Write about a situation in your life where you need faith
but have been viewing it through the lens of the flesh?
How can you shift to a faith-filled perspective?

Prayer: *Thank you, God, for increasing my faith in the most
difficult circumstances. Please help me to align my life with Your will,
God. Lord God, You know my heart and how difficult this trial is
in my life (you can talk about question 3 here), help me to increase
my faith. I thank You, God, for all you are changing within me. I
want to know Your heart, Lord. In the name of Jesus I pray, Amen.*

Day 5:
Trouble

The third root of doubt is **trouble**.

Don't be discouraged in your times of trouble. Instead, consider your times of trouble an opportunity for joy! Don't try to pray yourself out of the trouble without direction from the Lord—it could be your opportunity to grow your faith.

"Dear brothers and sisters, when troubles of any kind come your way, consider it an opportunity for great joy. For you know when your faith is tested, your endurance has a chance to grow. So let is grow, for when your endurance is fully developed, you will be perfect and complete, needing nothing." James 1:2-4 NLT

Let's get this out of the way early in the journey: being a disciple is not easy. The passage in James clearly indicates that we will face trouble—but those are the very moments when our faith is tested. Jesus knew it would not be easy. What He did for us on the cross was not easy, but He did it because of His love for us.

Thankfully, we are not left unprepared. Through the words of Jesus—and the whole Word of God—we are equipped. Jesus knew what we would face and still assured us that we could find peace in Him.

"I have told you all this so that you may have peace in me. Here on earth you will have many trials and sorrows. But take heart, because I have overcome the world."
John 16:33 NLT

Do we let trouble cause us to doubt God? **No.** We recognize where our strength comes from, and we endure to the very end. You don't stop having problems when you become a disciple—in fact, you enter into a war for your soul. Jesus warns us clearly:

"The thief's purpose is to steal and kill and destroy. My purpose is to give them a rich and satisfying life."
John 10:10 NLT

You were created in love, with purpose, and that purpose was placed in you from the very beginning by God.

"For we are God's masterpiece. He has created us anew in Christ Jesus, so we can do the good things He planned for us long ago."
Ephesians 2:10 NLT

The devil wants to destroy your purpose, your life, and the gift of eternal life that Jesus died to give you. The devil is going to do anything and everything to gain your soul. As disciples, we must be prepared to go to war—not only for ourselves, but for those who need Jesus—for the world.

"Stay alert! Watch out for your great enemy, the devil. He prowls around like a roaring lion, looking for someone to devour."
1 Peter 5:8 NLT

Discipleship

Scriptures: James 1:2-4, John 16:33, John 10:10,
Ephesians 2:10, 1 Peter 5:8
Additional Scriptures: 1 Peter 4:19, Isaiah 41:10, 2
Corinthians 12:9

Questions:

1. What is a situation in your life where you need the joy of
the Lord?

2. Is it hard for you to accept that God created you for a
purpose?

3. Where is the devil attacking you? What is the devil trying
to steal, kill, or destroy in your life?

Prayer: *Lord, show me joy in the smallest details of life. Make
Your presence real to me when I am at my worse. Pour Your oil of
gladness over me when I feel like I am in the dark. When the enemy
attacks me, please remind me that You are with me. Help me to
recognize who the enemy is and how the enemy seeks to attack me in
my life. I want to be Your masterpiece, mold me into who You want
me to be, my God. I want to bring glory to You, God. In the name of
my Savior, Jesus Christ, I pray. Amen.*

Day 6:
Walking by Faith

"For we walk by faith, not by sight."
2 Corinthians 5:7 ESV

As disciples, we see differently. Remember we do not see with our flesh—we fix our eyes on what we cannot see. I know that sounds confusing – how do we fix our eyes on something we cannot see? Jesus explains an essential part of walking in faith with the help of something unseen:

"I will ask the Father, and He will give you another Helper, so that He may be with you forever; the Helper is the Spirit of truth, whom the world cannot receive, because it does not see Him or know Him; but you know Him because He remains with you and will be in you."
John 14:16-17 NASB2020

We have a Helper inside of us—the Spirit of Truth, the Holy Spirit! When we choose to take the step of faith and believe in Jesus Christ (John 3:16), we receive the Holy Spirit indwelling within us. The Holy Spirit remains within us forever and becomes our Helper.

But how does the Holy Spirit help us walk by faith? What does the Spirit of Truth give us to fix our eyes on?

"But the Helper, the Holy Spirit whom the Father will send in My name, He will teach you all things, and remind you of all that I said to you."
— *Jesus*, John 14:26 NASB2020

The Holy Spirit will teach us—not just some things, but **all** things. What does that mean? Every single question you have, every concern, every issue in your life, every pain and hurt—every single thing can be brought to the Holy Spirit in Jesus' name. The Holy Spirit is our teacher, teaching us how to handle all our circumstances, and showing us how to find healing and peace in God. There is **nothing** that you will face, at any moment, that the Holy Spirit cannot teach you to overcome. Why? Because Jesus overcame the world (John 16:33).

The Holy Spirit will remind us of the Word of God. This passage should light a fire in every disciple to study the Word of God. Even when you are worried that you may not understand what you are reading in the Bible, this passage promises two things:

1. The Holy Spirit will **teach you** the verses you read but don't understand, and
2. Though you may think you won't remember what you read, the Holy Spirit will be there to **remind you** of the Word of God you have heard or read— even if you think you have forgotten it.

"It is the same with My word. I send it out, and it always produces fruit. It will accomplish all I want it to, and it will prosper everywhere I send it."
Isaiah 55:11 NLT

God promises that His Word will never return void. That means that, no matter what, if you are receiving His Word—whether by hearing, reading, studying, or listening—it has a purpose for your life. The Holy Spirit, who is with you all your life, will remind you of that Word exactly when you need it, whether it be last Sunday or years ago. That's the promise.

Our response, as disciples, is to study the Word of God and ask the Holy Spirit to teach us how to apply the Word in our lives. The Word of God is foundational in building our relationship with Jesus and necessary in refining who we are into who God created us to be. Through the Word, we learn the voice of God and present ourselves to Him as vessels, ready to share the truth with the world.

"Do your best to present yourself to God as one approved, a worker who has no need to be ashamed, rightly handling the word of truth."
2 Timothy 2:15 ESV

As disciples, we are called to trust in God, even when we don't understand what He is doing in our lives.

"Trust in the Lord with all your heart; do not depend on your own understanding. Seek His will in all you do, and he will show you which path to take."
Proverbs 3:5-6 NLT

Discipleship

Scriptures: 2 Corinthians 5:7, John 14:16-17, John 3:16, John 14:26, John 16:33, Isaiah 55:11, 2 Timothy 2:15, Proverbs 3:5-6
Additional Scriptures: Hebrews 11:6

Questions:

1. Have you felt the Holy Spirit before? If so, describe how you knew it was the presence of God. If not, take a moment to ask God to reveal Himself to you through the Holy Spirit—have faith!

2. How do you expect the Holy Spirit to instruct you when you are outside of the will of God?

3. How often have you read the Bible in the past? How do you plan on changing your Bible-reading habits?

Prayer: *Thank you God, for revealing Yourself through the Holy Spirit. I give my life to You, teach me how to walk in a way that pleases you my Lord, my God. Help me to recognize the moments the Holy Spirit is instructing me and help me to figure out how to apply Your Word to my life. When I stray away from You God, remind me that I need more of You. I thank You, my God, for Your grace.*

There is no one like You, Lord. In the beautiful name of Jesus, I pray. Amen.

Day 7:
Hearing God

John 10:3-5 NLT
"The gatekeeper opens the gate for him, and the sheep recognize his voice and come to him. He calls his own sheep by name and leads them out. After he has gathered his own flock, he walks ahead of them, and they follow him because they know his voice. They won't follow a stranger; they will run from him because they don't know his voice." – Jesus

Jesus taught this parable because He wanted those who follow Him to realize He is the Good Shepherd. A flock of sheep spends their days roaming the pastures with their shepherd. The sheep **know** who their shepherd is, they **know** his voice. In the same way, as disciples, we should **know our Shepherd's voice**.

"I am the good shepherd; I know my own sheep, and they know me." – Jesus, John 10:14 NLT

I know it's hard to pick up the Bible and stay with it—but it's worth it. Start off small: put everything else away for five minutes, pick up a physical Bible, and just read—five uninterrupted minutes. Then, gradually increase your time. I'm not concerned about whether you will eventually spend more time in Scripture, because once you open the door to that part of your relationship with God, you will find you can't go without it. God really does draw you in.

"Draw near to God, and He will draw near to you. Cleanse your hands, you sinners, and purify your hearts, you double-minded."
James 4:8 ESV

Remember, just like the father of the child with the demon (Day Three), we may not do it perfectly—but if we are sincere, the Lord sees us and honors our effort. The difficulty is in the beginning. We have to start somewhere. All I ask is that you pick up an actual Bible (the actual book, not the app on your device) and read it for five minutes daily for one week.

"That is why the Holy Spirit says, 'Today, when you hear his voice, don't harden your hearts as Israel did when they rebelled, when they tested me in the wilderness... Be careful then, dear brothers and sisters. Make sure that your own hearts are not evil and unbelieving, turning away from the living God."
Hebrews 3:7-8, 12 NLT

We hear many voices every day. Whether you are a spouse, a parent, a sibling, a friend, a coworker, or a part of a church family—voices are constantly speaking into your life. But you will recognize the voices of those closest to you, the ones you hear most often. I know my daughter's voice. I know my husband's voice. I hear them every day, I can tell you, with pretty good accuracy, what their opinion is on almost any subject. I know them.

As a disciple, I strive to know the voice of God in the same way—and to become like Him. That is how we are called to know Him.

Knowing the voice of God activates our faith. When we know the desires of His heart, we know what to pray—and *how to effectively* pray—because we are emboldened knowing that what we pray is going to happen because it's God will.

"But Peter said, 'I don't have any silver or gold for you. But I'll give you what I have. In the name of Jesus Christ the Nazarene, get up and walk!'"
Acts 3:6 NLT

Peter did not beg God to heal the lame man in Acts 3. Peter **knew** the heart of the Father. He knew that when he said, *"In the name of Jesus Christ of Nazareth, get up and walk,"* the man would walk. Peter had no doubt—he didn't question God's ability to heal or His willingness to do it. He walked with Jesus, daily—Peter **knew** what God would do in that moment.

Peter knew the Father well enough. Do we?

Discipleship

Scriptures: John 10:3-5, John 10:14, James 4:8, Hebrews 3:7-8 & 12, Acts 3:6
Additional Scriptures: Psalm 95:7, 2 Chronicles 8:14-15

Questions:

1. Do you know the voice of God? If so, how do you hear Him?

2. We are at the end of the first week—have your Bible-reading habits changed? If so, how?

3. Do you spend enough time with God to know His voice? If not, create a plan to spend more intentional time with your Father. He is waiting for you.

Prayer: *Father God, I thank You for loving me enough to draw me closer to You. I want to know You, God, I want to know Your voice. Please don't let me leave Your presence without having an encounter with You. God, You are my desire. Teach me, Oh Lord, how to pray Your will, show me Your desire for my life and for my generations. I give myself away to You, God. In the wonderful name of Jesus, I pray. Amen.*

Discipleship Group
Week 1

Additional Scriptures Shared with the Group:

Questions:

1. How has your understanding of what it means to be a true disciple changed through these 7 days?

2. How do you typically respond when your prayers are not answered the way you hoped? What does that reveal about your view of God's will?

3. How has your Bible reading changed this week, even if only slightly? What have you learned about yourself through that process?

Prayer Points:
- Identify and uproot any doubt.
- Increase in faith.
- Hearing the voice of God.

Day 8:
Expectations

Now that we know what faith looks like and how to learn to hear the voice of God, we need to know what to expect as a faith-filled disciple. There is a reason faith is central to our walk with God—if life became perfect after accepting Jesus Christ as our Savior, then we would not need faith. There would be no need for faith because everything would be great.

The Bible warns God's people of what to expect in their walk as disciples of Jesus Christ.

"I have told you all this so that you may have peace in me. Here on earth you will have many trials and sorrows. But take heart, because I have overcome the world."
-Jesus, John 16:33 NLT

Jesus prepared us, knowing that we would face difficulties in life—even as believers. But with Jesus Christ, we find peace. The peace is not that the trials disappear; the peace is that He died for us when we were still sinners. He loved us enough to take on our punishment of death and offer us eternal life in communion with Him.

"Dear friends, don't be surprised at the fiery trials you are going through, as if something strange were happening to you. Instead, be very glad—for these trials make you partners with Christ in his suffering, so that you will have the wonderful joy of seeing his glory when it is revealed to all the world."
1 Peter 4:12-13 NLT

There is a joy that overcomes every believer when they first accept Jesus Christ, but that joy can quickly be lost if you expect everyone around you—and every circumstance—to naturally reflect the same joy. The world is still lost, and the Word of God tells us to be alert:

"Stay alert! Watch out for your great enemy, the devil. He prowls around like a roaring lion, looking for someone to devour. Stand firm against him, and be strong in your faith. Remember that your family of believers all over the world is going through the same kind of suffering you are."
1 Peter 5:8-9 NLT

The enemy has one purpose—to destroy you. The enemy seeks to steal, kill, and destroy. The moment you choose to follow Jesus, you become more of a target than ever before. You are choosing to walk in the purpose you were created for by the Creator of the universe—the devil is mad.

But God prepares us. The Bible does not tell us there will be no valleys. Instead, the Word of God tells us not to fear when we walk through the valley of the shadow of death. God is not preparing us to walk through any small valley. I don't know a lot about valleys, but I feel like the valley of the shadow of death is probably one of the worst.

"Even though I walk through the valley of the shadow of death, I fear no evil, for You are with me; Your rod and Your staff, they comfort me."
Psalm 23:4 NASB2020

The promise is that God will be with us in the worst moments, comforting us. He also does not promise that there will never be terrors or arrows that fly at us. Instead, God tells us that those evils will not touch us.

"Do not be afraid of the terrors of the night, nor the arrow that flies in the day... Though a thousand fall at your side, though ten thousand are dying around you, these evils will not touch you."
Psalm 91:5,7 NLT

The difficult circumstances—the worst moments in your life, the troubles, and the tribulations—are the times when our faith in God is put to work. In the tribulations, we grow into who God wants us to be. In the trials, we learn what God's voice sounds like. And in the worst moments, we find the joy of having a Savior, because those are the times when we truly need Him. We grow into understanding who God is in every season of our lives.

"Dear brothers and sisters, when troubles of any kind come your way, consider it an opportunity for great joy. For you know that when your faith is tested, your endurance has a chance to grow. So let it grow, for when your endurance is fully developed, you will be perfect and complete needing nothing."
James 1:2-4 NLT

Faith in the worst moment of our lives build us into warriors, ready for spiritual battle. When we face the hardest battles and come out on the other side, we give God the opportunity to show us how He truly makes all things work together for the good of those who believe in Him. Then we realize—He genuinely is all we need.

Discipleship

Scriptures: John 16:33, 1 Peter 4:12-13, 1 Peter 5:8-9,
Psalm 23:4, Psalm 91:5 & 7, James 1:2-4
Additional Scriptures: Revelation 14:12, 1 Peter 1:6

Questions:

1. What is the most terrifying experience in your life? Do
you remember how you saw God with you in that
moment?

2. Can you write about a time you grew spiritually because
you passed through a tribulation? If so, explain that
growth—how did it make you better for God's Kingdom?
If not, what do you think would be a good area for
spiritual growth for you?

3. What is an event or trial you experienced that you
thought was really bad, but ended up working out for your
good?

Prayer: *God, please show me where You are in the trials I face.
Show me, Father, where I need to grow in my walk with You. Lead
me in my darkest valleys, teach me to rely on You and trust in You.
Show me, God, the good all things. I humbly give You all of me. In
Jesus' name, I pray. Amen*

Day 9:
Armor of God

Ephesians 6:11-12 NLT
"Put on all of God's armor so that you will be able to stand firm against all strategies of the devil. For we are not fighting against flesh-and-blood enemies, but against evil rulers and authorities of the unseen world, against mighty powers in this dark world, and against evil spirits in the heavenly places."

God's love for us is so great that He does not just warn us about the trials we will face as disciples—He also gives us clear instructions on how we need to face those tribulations. In Ephesians, the Lord warns that our fights are not against the people around us. **The battles are against spirits of darkness that we cannot see!** No, not ghost—these are demonic spirits with the sole purpose of destroying you. But with the full armor of God, you can stand firm against *ALL* strategies of the devil!

The Armor
"Therefore, put on every piece of God's armor so you will be able to resist the enemy in the time of evil. Then after the battle you will still be standing firm."
Ephesians 6:13 NLT

Prepare. God does not speak in vain. Every word He gives us—in Scripture, prophetically, and through other spiritual gifts—is for a purpose.

"I publicly proclaim bold promises. I do not whisper obscurities in some dark corner; I would not have told the people of Israel to seek me if I could not be found. I, the Lord, speak only what is true and declare only what is right."
Isaiah 45:19 NLT

Therefore, if God instructs us to prepare for battle by putting on the armor of God—and that is how we stand firm—then we thank God for the warning and rise up, placing the armor on daily, ready to confront the enemy! It's time for war.

Belt of Truth
"Jesus told him, 'I am the way, the truth, and the life. No one can come to the Father except through me.'"
John 14:6 NLT

The truth of what Jesus did for you—and who Jesus is to you—will always be the point the enemy will try to use to confuse you. The devil wants to destroy you. If the devil can keep you stuck in shame, guilt, and sinful habits, then he robs you of the true freedom Jesus came to give you through the power of the Holy Spirit living inside of you. You must believe what Jesus says about you. That truth is what holds the rest of the armor together.

Breastplate of Righteousness
"Those who are dominated by the sinful nature think about sinful things, but those who are controlled by the Holy Spirit think about things that please the Spirit. So letting your sinful nature control your mind leads to death. But letting the Spirit control your minds leads to life and peace. For the sinful nature is always hostile to God. It never

did obey God's laws, and it never will. That's why those who are still under the control of their sinful nature can never please God."
Romans 8:5-8 NLT

Jesus became the offering for our sin so that we could be made right with God through Christ (2 Corinthians 5:21). When we were made right with God, Jesus sent us the Holy Spirit to dwell within us. If we allow the Holy Spirit to dominate our lives, we live led by the One who is truly righteous. He drapes us in a robe of righteousness (Isaiah 61:10). The breastplate protects the most vital organs. When we allow sin to creep into our lives or into the lives of our families, we open a door to the enemy—and that affects our lives and the lives of our future generations.

"But seek first the kingdom of God and his righteousness, and all these things will be added to you."
Matthew 6:33 ESV

God promises that if we seek His Kingdom and live righteously before anything else, we will have everything we need. This verse in Matthew confirms that God knows we are capable of living righteously through Holy Spirit— and when we do, that righteousness becomes our breastplate in spiritual warfare. The breastplate of righteousness protects us from the deepest wounds—the wounds that kill our purpose, kill our joy, and destroy our lives.

Gospel of Peace on Feet
We must stand firm on the peace of God. Sometimes you find yourself standing in a hospital room, sometimes at a funeral, sometimes reading the bills you cannot pay, or in an office turning in a job application. Wherever you are standing, your feet should be standing on the peace of Jesus Christ.

"Don't worry about anything; instead, pray about everything. Tell God what you need, and thank him for all he has done. Then you will experience God's peace, which exceeds anything we can understand. His peace will guard your hearts and minds as you live in Christ Jesus."
Philippians 4:6-7 NLT

The enemy wants to shake your faith—often through fear. The peace of God will keep you standing firm in your faith. Lace up your boots daily with Jesus' gospel of peace.

Shield of Faith
"Faith means being sure of the things we hope for. And faith means knowing that something is real even if we do not see it."
Hebrews 11:1 ICB

We know what faith is and what it looks like in our lives. But how does it shield us? As we are attacked by the enemy, faith is how we see our victory. We may be in a valley surrounded by darkness, death, and armies against us—but faith shields us from being consumed by what we see. Instead, in faith, we see our great God who can do all things—even the impossible.

You must learn to actively see in the spiritual realm and blind yourself to what the flesh sees. Before accepting Jesus Christ as Savior, we could only see in the flesh. But the Holy Spirit opens our eyes to who Jesus is and what He can do in us and through us.

"Satan, who is the god of this world, has blinded the minds of those who don't believe. They are unable to see the glorious light of the Good News. They don't understand this message about the glory of Christ, who is the exact likeness of God."
2 Corinthians 4:4 NLT

When you see through faith, it becomes a shield that

protects your mind from every attack of the enemy.

Helmet of Salvation

"Salvation is not a reward for the good things we have done, so none of us can boast about it. For we are God's masterpiece, He has created us anew in Christ Jesus, so we can do the good things He planned for us long ago."
Ephesians 2:9-10 NLT

The battle within our minds is one of the hardest battles to fight against the enemy. When we believe the thoughts that attack us, the enemy paralyzes us. We cannot reach the purpose God created us for when we are stuck in fear, or guilt, or shame.

God sent Jesus to die for us so we could have the freedom to do His will. We need to remember—we were purchased at the highest cost. The King of the universe found value in us. When we place the helmet of salvation on and recognize that value, we raise a shield against the doubts, thoughts, and lies the enemy plants in our minds.

"For you know that God paid a ransom to save you from the empty life you inherited from your ancestors. And it was not paid with mere gold or silver, which lose their value. It was the precious blood of Christ, the sinless, spotless Lamb of God."
1 Peter 1:18-19 NLT

My empty life meant so much to God that He took it on the cross with Him and gave me the precious gift of His blood. If we can just remember that, then the lies of the enemy will fall against the helmet of salvation Jesus Christ has tenderly placed on our heads.

Discipleship

Scriptures: Ephesians 6:11-12, Ephesians 6:13, Isaiah 45:19, John 14:6, Romans 8:5-8, 2 Corinthians 5:21, Matthew 6:33, Philippians 4:6-7, Hebrews 11:1, 2 Corinthians 4:4, Ephesians 2:9-10, 1 Peter 1:18-19
Additional Scriptures: Psalm 35:1-2

Questions:

1. What is something you have heard over and over again about God that you never really made the effort to understand—maybe it's a verse someone always quotes or something preached often? Write it down and take 5 minutes to dwell on what that verse or teaching means in the Kingdom of God.

2. How do you define truth? What is your ultimate truth? What does it mean to let Jesus decide what truth is in your life? Create a plan to make Jesus the ultimate judge of truth in your daily life.

3. Is there something in your life that you see as extremely bad and you find it difficult to have faith in? Write out a faith statement, boldly declaring in faith how God is going to have the victory and glory in this situation.

Prayer: *My God, thank You for preparing me for the spiritual war. I want to glorify You in every moment of battle and take the territory* *for Your Kingdom, God. Open my ears, Oh God, to hear Your voice and to store Your declarations in my heart. I want to hear every word You speak to me, and I want to meditate on Your instruction, Father. Point me in the direction of Your truth in every situation, fill me with Your peace in every battle, lead me down the righteous path, I submit my doubts to You God. Help me to see when and how You move in my life as I grow in my faith. I am humbled that You found value in saving me and I hold onto that salvation, as my protection from attacks of the enemy. Thank You for it all, in the mighty name of Jesus, I pray. Amen.*

Day 10:
The Bridegroom

Honestly, it is extremely difficult to recognize the voice of the Father—God—if you do not read His Word. I understand there are fellow believers around the world who do not have access to the Scriptures, and God uses different avenues for His Word to be heard in those places. But for the majority of people in the Western Hemisphere, the Word of God is readily available and seldom read—apart from the few verses shared during a weekly church service.

"For husbands, this means love your wives, just as Christ loved the church. He gave up his life for her."
Ephesians 5:25 NLT

There are many references to the church being the bride and Jesus Christ being our Bridegroom: Revelation 19:6-9, Isaiah 62:5, Matthew 25:1-13, Jeremiah 2:2, Ephesians 5:25-27, and Song of Solomon.

"For your Creator will be your husband; the Lord of Heaven's Armies is his name! He is your Redeemer; the Holy One of Israel,

the God of all the earth."
Isaiah 54:5 NLT

Sometimes, we miss the importance of God's description of us as the bride to Christ Jesus. We go and sit in a seat on a Sunday, maybe at a mid-week service, and we call ourselves "Christians." Christians because we go to church twice a week. But if we take the description from the Bible and apply it, then right now, in this moment, we are preparing for a great wedding with King Jesus.

I don't know about you but before I married my husband, I talked to him—a lot. To some, we talked too much; my mom would have to come out of her room and run him out of the house because he stayed too long. Even now, after being together for 20 years, people still tell us we talk too much—but we are happy, we are best friends, and we know each other more than anyone else in the world.

Should it not be the same in our relationship with God? If God compares us to a bride, should we not spend as much time as possible getting to know our Bridegroom—the One we are going to be with for eternity? What would happen if you only spent an hour or two per week with your significant other? What would happen if the only communication you had with your spouse was on a Monday morning from 10 a.m. to 12 p.m.? (Some services are even shorter than that.) Would you even consider that a marriage? No, of course not. Why do we apply a different standard to our Bridegroom, who died for us to spend eternity with Him?

"Never stop praying."
1 Thessalonians 5:17 NLT

This scripture is short and simple, but it conveys the desire of our Father to be in constant communication with Him.

There are no parameters around this verse. God does not limit "never stop praying" to certain situations, the words do not apply only to the worst circumstances. No. The Word of God tells us to never stop praying—meaning prayer should be our lifestyle. We should talk to the Lord at all times, at every moment. God should be in every breath, every beat of our heart, and in every thought.

When we are in constant communication with God, His Word is hidden in our hearts as a reminder of what pleases the Lord (Psalm 119:11) and as a reminder of what we need to cut out of our lives to live according to the Holy Spirit (Romans 8:5).

Discipleship

Scriptures: Ephesians 5:25, Revelation 19:6-9, Isaiah 62:5, Matthew 25:1-13, Jeremiah 2:2, Ephesians 5:25-27, Isaiah 54:5, 1 Thessalonians 5:17, Psalm 119:11, Romans 8:5
Additional Scriptures: Song of Solomon

Questions:

1. How much time have you spent with God this past week, either in the Bible or in prayer? Is that time adequate for the King of Kings and Lord of Lords? If not, identify what keeps you from time with Jesus daily.

2. What does a healthy marriage look like to you? It may be difficult to comprehend God's love for His bride—the Church—if we were raised in an unhealthy home with a poor example of marriage. Compare and contrast what Jesus' love looks like for the Church, His bride, compared to marriages you have witnessed.

3. What changes can you start making today to cultivate the Bride and Bridegroom relationship with Jesus? What does that mean to you?

Prayer: *Father God, thank You for Your revelation and Your love. Help me, Lord, to identify distractions in my life that keep me* *from You. I ask You, God, to bring conviction to those areas of my life that I need to separate from to make room for You, God. Help me to understand the love You have for me and show me what a true relationship looks like in You. I want my life to overflow with abundant joy, teach me how to be in relationship with You, so that our relationship overflows into my family life. Please forgive me for the times I forget to come to You with my needs, I commit myself to You, God from today forward. Holy Spirit guide me on the narrow path. In the powerful name of Jesus, I pray. Amen.*

Day 11:
The Sword of the Spirit

"For the word of God is alive and powerful. It is sharper than the sharpest two-edged sword, cutting between soul and spirit, between joint and marrow. It exposes our innermost thoughts and desires."
Hebrews 4:12 NLT

God has a reason for wanting us to be in constant communication with Him, and a reason for us to know His Word and His voice. It is God who exposes that which needs to be refined within us. Our flesh was born in opposition to the Spirit of God, but when we are born again, our spirit begins to fight the flesh in order to align us with God's purpose. The Word of God reveals our weaknesses, allowing us to recognize what needs to be changed through the strength of the Holy Spirit.

"Each time [the Lord] said, 'My grace is all you need. My power works best in weakness.' So now I am glad to boast about my weaknesses, so that the power of Christ can work through me. That's why I take pleasure in my weaknesses, and in the insults, hardships, persecutions, and troubles that I suffer for Christ. For when I am weak, then I am strong."
2 Corinthians 12: 9-10 NLT

God loves to expose. But for us, exposure can be a difficult process to endure. It is the nature of the flesh to not want to be flawed. Yet, the nature of the Holy Spirit is to expose and refine. God wants the best for you, and that means removing the worst from you. God never wanted any circumstance to hinder your purpose in Him.

"I have refined you, but not as silver is refined. Rather, I have refined you in the furnace of suffering."
Isaiah 48:10 NLT

God knows that in the suffering you have endured, a refining process has taken place. But it was never the Lord's intention for you to delay His purpose because of the difficulties you have experienced.

"And we know that God causes everything to work together for the good of those who love God and are called according to His purpose for them."
Romans 8:28 NLT

The Sword of the Spirit—God's Word—comes to cut the lies of the enemy from your life. Scripture is a powerful testimony to you because it is God's love letter filled with promises for all the good that He wants for you, despite the evil you have seen in the world.

The Sword of the Spirit also works powerfully to expose the lies of the devil in the lives of those who hear the truth of the gospel through you. However, Scripture is clear in explaining that the truth may not always be well received.

"Do you think I have come to bring peace to the earth? No, I have come to divide people against each other! From now on families will be split apart, three in favor of me, and two against—or two in favor and three against."
-Jesus, Luke 12:51-52 NLT

In true sword-like fashion, the truth of the gospel may divide where we expect it to unite. We may lose the people closest to us—not because of Jesus—but because the world is blind to the lovingkindness of our God. The Word of God clearly indicates that all people know the truth.

"They know the truth about God because he has made it obvious to them. For ever since the world was created, people have seen the earth and sky. Through everything God made, they can clearly see his invisible qualities—his eternal power and divine nature. So they have no excuse for not knowing God."
Romans 1:19-20 NLT

True love is not forced. The moment someone truly encounters our Savior, Jesus Christ, God stirs something within them that allows them to recognize the presence of the Holy Spirit. Unbelief is not natural, not even in the flesh, because God has created all people with the capacity to recognize Him through creation. Unbelief is from the devil. The Sword of the Spirit cuts away the lies—like unbelief—from your life. The sword is the tool that cuts in order to set you apart for His purpose.

Discipleship

Scriptures: Hebrews 4:12, 2 Corinthians 12: 9-10, Isaiah 48:10, Romans 8:28, Luke 12:51-52, Romans 1:19-20
Additional Scriptures: 2 Timothy 3:16-17

Questions:

1. Can you identify your weaknesses? List the areas of flesh in your life that need refining through the Holy Spirit.

2. How have the weaknesses in question 1 hindered your walk with God, or how might they hinder your walk in the future?

3. Has the Word of God ever cut you like a double-edged sword? If so, what Scripture pierced you? If not, has there been any Scripture in this study so far that made you react strongly? Explain.

Prayer: *God, help me to recognize areas of my life that need more of You. Help me in my weaknesses (list your answers from question 1). I give myself to You, Lord—refine me. Forgive me for the times my weaknesses have affected my walk with You. Continue to pierce my heart with Your word. I love You, Lord and I give myself away to You. In the powerful name of Jesus, I pray. Amen.*

Day 12:
Spiritual Warfare

2 Corinthians 10:3-5 NLT
"We are human, but we don't wage war as humans do. We use God's mighty weapons, not worldly weapons, to knock down the strongholds of human reasoning and to destroy false arguments. We destroy every proud obstacle that keeps people from knowing God. We capture their rebellious thoughts and teach them to obey Christ."

One of the most difficult parts of discipleship is recognizing spiritual warfare. An argument with your significant other, an offensive comment that hurts you, or an action by a stranger that angers you—these are all tactics the enemy uses.

"Be sober-minded; be watchful. Your adversary the devil prowls around like a roaring lion, seeking someone to devour."
1 Peter 5:8 ESV

A disciple should be on alert daily, because the devil wants to destroy you. Every moment you are not glorifying God or focused on His desires, you are opening up the door for the devil to tempt you with your own evil desires. Your mind must remain fixed on the things of God's Kingdom at all times (Colossians 3:2).

"And remember, when you are being tempted, do not say, 'God is tempting me.' God is never tempted to do wrong, and he never tempts anyone else. Temptation comes from our own desires, which entice us and drag us away. These desires give birth to sinful actions. And when sin is allowed to grow, it gives birth to death."
James 1:13-15 NLT

As a disciple, you must guard your mind from those desires that are contrary to God's Kingdom. Desires not rooted in His will are the very desires that lead us into sin. So how do we know if our desires are aligned with God's desires? We measure them against the Word of God.

"My people will be destroyed because they have no knowledge. You priests have refused to learn. So I will refuse to let you be priests to me. You have forgotten the teachings of your God. So I will reject your children."
Hosea 4:6 ICB

Another version of the passage in Hosea begins *with "My people are being destroyed because they don't know Me"* (NLT). God has given His people an entire book—a book that is regarded with a high degree of textual integrity in comparison to any other ancient manuscript. There is no valid reason not to read the Bible. Before we pursue spiritual gifts, before accepting another person's teaching or preaching, or before blindly obeying any leader, we must read the Word of God ourselves. The Bible contains eyewitness accounts of the words of Jesus—how can you claim to love your Savior and not want to read what He has already said?

As a disciple, you must not become caught up in the trends within Christianity—whether it's deliverance, prophetic words, prophetic worship, or teachings that focus on helping people become the best versions of themselves. All of it should revolve around Jesus Christ. It is His blood that delivers. It is the Holy Spirit that moves in the prophetic. It is God who transforms us into who He created us to be.

Too often, we focus so much on what we think we need to do for God's Kingdom that we get in the way of what God actually wants to do. We are called to be vessels for His will. But we can only be vessels if we truly submit to His will. **Otherwise, we will end up chasing our will for God, rather than His will for us.**

Discipleship

Scriptures: 2 Corinthians 10:3-5, 1 Peter 5:8, Colossians 3:2, James 1:13-15, Hosea 4:6
Additional Scriptures: Ephesians 6:18, Song of Solomon 3:8

Questions:

1. Identify areas in your life that were actually spiritual warfare, but you did not recognize the attack—and instead reacted in the flesh.

2. Identify times throughout your day where you are not really thinking about God or the things of His Kingdom. Create a plan to help you stay mindful of God during your day—use specific strategies like visible reminders, phone alerts, or having the Bible visible at all times.

3. Describe a time where you thought you were doing something for the Kingdom of God but later realized you were in the way of what God wanted to do. If you don't have an example, explain how you *could* unintentionally interfere with God's will. Then, set and describe boundaries to help prevent that from happening in the future.

Prayer: *Thank You, Lord, for the moments of my life that strengthened me in my relationship with You. Help me, Lord, to fight my battles with Your armor. I lay down my flesh and commit to reacting with Your Holy Spirit. Holy Spirit remind me throughout the day when my focus shifts from You to the world—let my life revolve around You. Accept my life, God, as a sacrifice to You. Refine me to a sweet aroma at Your throne. In the majestic name of Jesus, I pray. Amen.*

Day 13:
Spirit of Fear

2 Timothy 1:7 ESV
"For God gave us a spirit not of fear but of power and love and self-control."

Even people who do not know Christ will tell you that fear will always hold you back. First, we must acknowledge the weight that fear carries. If those who do not know God can see the strength of fear in their own lives—and if God reminds us over and over again to not fear—then we must be wise and recognize that fear can affect our faith if we allow it. God is telling us to be alert to fear and to know that fear is not from Him.

"Dear friends, do not believe everyone who claims to speak by the Spirit. You must test them to see if the spirit they have comes from God. For there are many false prophets in the world."
1 John 4:1 NLT

Second, we cannot deny the existence of evil spirits, and we must be able to recognize when evil spirits are attacking us. The passage in 2nd Timothy refers to fear as a spirit—a spirit that God does not give. If God did not give the spirit of fear, then who did? The devil.

"Jesus summoned His twelve disciples and gave them authority over unclean spirits, to cast them out, and to heal every disease and every sickness."
Matthew 10:1 NASB2020

As disciples, we have the authority to cast out the evil, unclean spirits. For that reason, we must learn God's desires in order to recognize what is unclean, unholy, and evil—and cast out all that is against the Kingdom of God.

"When an evil spirit leaves a person, it goes into the desert, seeking rest but finding none. Then it says, 'I will return to the person I came from.' So it returns and finds its former home empty, swept, and in order. Then the spirit finds seven other spirits more evil than itself, and they all enter the person and live there. And so that person is worse off than before. That will be the experience of this evil generation."
- *Jesus*, Matthew 12:43-45 NLT

Jesus warns us that evil spirits are capable of entering a person and leaving—comparing a person to a house. The comparison is clear: even when the evil spirit leaves, it can return with even more evil spirits if the house (the person) is empty. As a disciple, you need to be filled with the Holy Spirit constantly; otherwise, we leave ourselves open to the evil the enemy wants to use to destroy us.

"But I am not surprised! Even Satan disguises himself as an angel of light. So it is no wonder that his servants also disguise themselves as servants of righteousness. In the end they will get the punishment their wicked deeds deserve."
2 Corinthians 11:14-15 NLT

The Word of God warns us throughout Scripture that we

are subject to demonic influence and there are evil spirits that act, look, and seem to be righteous. These types of evil spirits can confuse a believer who does not know the voice of God. A small and subtle deviation from God's true voice can be difficult to catch for someone who does not read their Bible, is not filled with the Holy Spirit, or is being influenced by a lying, evil spirit. Discipleship requires commitment to this walk of faith to truly receive the freedom Jesus died to give us.

Discipleship

Scriptures: 2 Timothy 1:7, 1 John 4:1, Matthew 10:1, Matthew 12:43-45, 2 Corinthians 11:14-15
Additional Scriptures: Psalm 118:5-6

Questions:

1. What fears do you have? Identify the fears the enemy uses to attack you. List them and submit them to God.

2. What is unclean, unholy, or evil in your life? List these things below, and begin to tell God that you no longer want any part of them. Ask God to break them off of you by the blood of Jesus Christ, our Savior.

3. Create a plan to keep your house full of the Holy Spirit—not just your physical home, but your spiritual temple: your body, your mind, and your spirit.

Prayer: *In the name of Jesus, I come against every fear that attacks my mind. I cast out the spirit of fear by the blood of Jesus, the devil no longer has a hold on me in these areas (list answers from question 1). Thank You, Jesus for Your freedom in my life. I break off every unsanctified area in my life by the authority of my Savior, Jesus Christ (list answers from question 2). Holy Spirit, You are welcome* *in my home and in every area of my life—fill me. Teach me. I am Yours. In the powerful name of Jesus, I pray. Amen.*

Day 14:
Authority

"But Jesus reprimanded him. 'Be quiet! Come out of the man,' he ordered. At that, the evil spirit screamed, threw the man into a convulsion, and then came out of him. Amazement gripped the audience, and they began to discuss what had happened. 'What sort of new teaching is this?' they asked excitedly. 'It has such authority! Even evil spirits obey his orders!'"
Mark 1:25-27 NLT

Jesus exercised His authority to cast out evil spirits throughout the New Testament. Jesus confronted demons—and as disciples, we are called to do the same. He did not allow the demon to influence His authority— He called out the evil spirit. As disciples, we cannot ignore demons, Jesus taught us that evil spirits cannot control whether we do the will of the Father. The Father wants people whole, and Jesus called us, as disciples, to act in alignment with God's will.

"Heal the sick, raise the dead, cure those with leprosy, and cast out demons. Give as freely as you have received!"
Matthew 10:8 NLT

As disciples, we must recognize the power and authority that Jesus has given us. The easiest way to walk in that authority is by learning the heart of the Father. When we know the heart of God and His will, our love for Him grows into the desire to obey Him (John 14:15).

"Look, I have given you authority over all the power of the enemy, and you can walk among snakes and scorpions and crush them. Nothing will injure you. But don't rejoice because evil spirits obey you, rejoice because your names are registered in heaven."
Luke 10:19-20 NLT

God's will for His people to walk in freedom is so strong that He has given us this authority over any and all power of the enemy. There is no reason to fear any evil spirit, but every reason to cast out any evil spirit you encounter. We demonstrate the love of Christ by loving one another—and what greater love is there than showing everyone you encounter the healing and freedom Jesus offers?

"Your love for one another will prove to the world that you are my disciples."
John 13:35 NLT

Allowing someone to walk in destruction is not love—especially when you know the One who can end that destruction and bring life. Love means sharing the fruits of the Spirit with everyone you encounter and pouring out the same love the Holy Spirit rains on you in your time of intimacy with the Lord.

Discipleship

Scriptures: Mark 1:25-27, Matthew 10:8, John 14:15, Luke 10:19-20, John 13:35
Additional Scriptures: Matthew 10:1, Luke 9:1

Questions:

1. When Jesus cast out the demon in Mark chapter 1, the man with the evil spirit screamed and convulsed before the demon came out. The Word of God gives us an experience of deliverance by Jesus to set our expectations. How did you view deliverance before reading about how Jesus casted out demons, and has your view changed after seeing how Jesus delivered people? If so, how?

2. List any areas of demonic oppression you want Jesus to free you from. Then, cast out the demons that you have struggled with in the name of Jesus—just as Jesus commanded the demon to leave in Mark chapter 1.

3. Create a plan for how you could confront the demons that destruct the lives of those you love most.

Prayer: *Father God, I thank You for bringing revelation into my life. I thank You, God, for Your blood and Your power freeing my life. I cast out every demonic influence in my life in the powerful name* *of Jesus. I cast out: (list from question 2) by the blood of Jesus, who died for me and in His authority. I thank You, Lord Jesus for Your deliverance. I pray for discernment to recognize those around me who need Your freedom Jesus. I am a willing vessel for the will of You, My Father. In the name of my Almighty Savior, Jesus, I pray. Amen.*

Discipleship Group
Week 2

Additional Scriptures Shared with the Group:

Questions:

1. How has fear held you back from doing something you knew God was calling you to do?

2. Why do you think some believers hesitate to talk about spiritual warfare or casting out demons—even though Jesus made it a core part of ministry?

3. Have you ever mistaken something as being from God that, in hindsight, was spiritually deceptive? What helped you realize the truth?

Prayer Points:
- The Armor of God.
- Deliverance from demonic oppression.
- Deliverance from fear.

Day 15:
Fruits of the Spirit

"But the Holy Spirit produces this kind of fruit in our lives: love, joy, peace, patience, kindness, goodness, faithfulness, gentleness, and self-control. There is no law against these things!"
Galatians 5:22-23 NLT

These are the fruits we share with others to show who Christ is in our lives—and who He can be in theirs. We know that casting out evil spirits brings joy, peace, and goodness into someone's life. There is no reason to leave someone with a demon that brings the opposite of God's Kingdom into their life. Bringing the healing of Jesus into someone's life is kind and good. On the contrary, leaving someone in pain and suffering is harsh.

"You have not taken care of the weak. You have not tended the sick or bound up the injured. You have not gone looking for those who have wandered away and are lost. Instead, you have ruled them with harshness and cruelty."
Ezekiel 34:4 NLT

Those who are demonically influenced, sick, or weak need

to be cared for by those around them who know how to fight on the spiritual battlefield. The natural response to sickness, addiction, pain, habitual sin, and other demonic influences should always be freedom in Jesus. That freedom is brought by speaking the words God has given us the authority to use—to bring healing and deliverance through casting out demons.

"'Son of man, prophesy against the shepherds, the leaders of Israel. Give them this message from the Sovereign Lord: What sorrow awaits you shepherds who feed yourselves instead of your flocks. Shouldn't shepherds feed their sheep?'"
Ezekiel 34:2 NLT

Jesus showed us the ultimate act of humility by coming down from Heaven and giving His perfect self for sinners like us. His Kingdom goes against everything our flesh desires in this world. The "self" fights for its desires, wants, and what it *believes* to be needs. But God's Kingdom is upside-down: the last shall be first, and we must serve as Jesus did.

"For even the Son of Man came not to be served but to serve others and to give His life as a ransom for many."
Mark 10:45 NLT

There are promises throughout the Word of God for His people. That means it is pointless to hoard God's goodness for yourself. You do not have to worry about your needs or desires—especially not above the needs of others. You have God. He's going to take care of you. That's the promise. And that promise allows you to pour out the oil God pours into you—into others. This is how you become a living sacrifice unto the Lord.

Discipleship

Scriptures: Galatians 5:22-23, Ezekiel 34:4, Ezekiel 34:2, Mark 10:45
Additional Scriptures: John 15:8

Questions:

1. List the fruits of the Spirit from Galatians 5:22-23 that you struggle to share with others in your daily life.

2. What has been your natural response to sickness, addiction, pain, habitual sin, or other demonic influences? Have you intentionally considered how you respond to these types of attacks from the enemy?

3. In a world where you are taught to protect "self" flipping that concept upside-down to reflect the Kingdom of God can be difficult. Confront the actions you have taken to protect your 'self.' List those actions and then submit them to God.

Prayer: *Father God, I humbly come before You today grateful for the love, joy, peace, patience, kindness, goodness, faithfulness, gentleness, and self-control the Holy Spirit produces in me. Help me, my God, in the areas where I struggle to produce Your fruits. Teach me how to respond like You, Lord, when the enemy attacks me.*

Humble me, oh Lord, when I put myself before You. I submit all of myself to You, God, I know You know me better than anyone else and I relinquish my control to You. Help me to recognize when things that are happening are a God thing, even if it is against my desires. Thank you for Your grace, God. In Your mighty name I pray, Jesus. Amen.

Day 16:
Obedience

Luke 6:46 NLT
"So why do you keep calling me 'Lord, Lord!' when you don't do what I say?" – Jesus

Well, that's direct. Yes, we are saved by faith, but we are also called to be set apart, sanctified, and obedient. Jesus compares obedience to building a house on a solid rock foundation—a foundation that will stand firm in the worst circumstances, a house that will endure rising floodwaters. Disobedience, Jesus warns, is like building a home with no foundation—a home that will collapse into ruins in a flood (Luke 6:48-49).

"If you love me, obey my commandments."
-Jesus, John 14:15 NLT

This scripture is not saying God only loves you if you obey His commands. There can be confusion when teaching that obedience is birthed out of your love for God. Teaching and adhering to obedience to God's Word is not legalistic nor religious. **Obedience is a response to the heart of God.**

Many Christians compare teachings about obedience, avoidance of sin, and the fear of God to the teachings of the Pharisees, arguing that the grace of God covers all sin—continuous and habitual—because humans are not perfect. Yet, Jesus says:

"Therefore you shall be perfect, as your heavenly Father is perfect."
– Jesus, Matthew 5:48 NLT

There are one or two translations of the word *teleios* ('perfect' in this context) that may allow you to interpret the word to fit your sin. However, you shouldn't. Many verses speak to the struggle against sin; God acknowledges that victory over sin may take an entire lifetime— ultimately achieving victory in eternity. Yet Jesus did not speak these words in vain. His standard was given, not as a blatant demand for some unachievable goal, but as a standard to strive for—not for Him, but for us. A life lived in obedience gives us every tool in the Kingdom to withstand every situation. And Jesus knew it would be hard—that is why He gave us the Helper, the Holy Spirit.

"No, O people, the Lord has told you what is good, and this is what He requires of you: to do what is right, to love mercy, and to walk humbly with your God."
Micah 6:8 NLT

It is not obedience that makes you like the Pharisees. It is obedience taken to the point of doing the wrong thing. For example, healing is right in the Kingdom of God. But to the Pharisees, healing on a Sabbath was wrong. The rule for the Sabbath took precedence over doing what is right for the Kingdom of God—healing God's people.

"But the leader in charge of the synagogue was indignant that Jesus had healed her on the Sabbath day. 'There are six days of the week for working,' he said to the crowd. 'Come on those days to be healed, not on the Sabbath.'"
Luke 13:14 NLT

It is not obedience that makes you like the Pharisees. It is obedience without mercy. The Pharisees wanted to stone the woman caught in adultery because that was the law of Moses. Jesus showed mercy.

"They kept demanding an answer, so he stood up again and said, 'All right, but let the one who has never sinned throw the first stone!'"
John 8:7 NLT

Not one of them threw a stone. The only person with the authority to condemn the woman was the one without sin—Jesus. Yet He was the first to defend and save the accused, just as He saved us from our sin on the cross.

"Then Jesus stood up again and said to the woman, 'Where are your accusers? Didn't even one of them condemn you?' 'No, Lord,' she said. And Jesus said, 'Neither do I. Go and sin no more.'"
John 8:10-11 NLT

Jesus saved the accused, but we cannot ignore His parting words: *"Go and sin no more."* Jesus knew the future. He knew He would die on the cross for the sins of humanity, including the sin of the adulteress. If she continued sinning, He knew she would have access to forgiveness through His death and resurrection. Still, He told her to sin no more.

It is not obedience that makes you like the Pharisees. It is obedience with pride—obedience without humility. Humility is having a humble view of your value and importance. Yes, it means lowering your view of yourself. Be careful about how that statement makes you feel. The flesh sometimes reacts defensively, feeling as if someone is trying to bring you down. But we must view humility spiritually, without letting the enemy stir a fleshly desire to *be* someone. Our Savior came to the world in humility and meekness, and though He is greater than all, He took on the work of a servant. As His creation, Jesus must be the most important focus in our lives.

"Then He said to the crowd, 'If any of you wants to be my follower, you must give up your own way, take up your cross daily, and follow me. If you try to hang on to your life, you will lose it. But if you give up your life for my sake, you will save it."
Luke 9:23-24 NLT

Our "self," our flesh has no value—that is why we must give it up. If it had value, Jesus would have said, embrace yourself and be the best version of you. Instead, our old self is crucified with Jesus so that our body of sin is brought to nothing (Romans 6:6). We are valuable because we were created by God, for God, and saved by Jesus. That is our value. When you see yourself through God's purpose, God becomes the only thing that matters.

Pride takes on another form: greed. We want. We want—money, homes, cars, weddings, vacations, fine dining, the latest tech, and, to top it off… mansions in heaven. But how do we see our Savior Jesus washing the feet of His disciples and still desire things that have nothing to do with the heart of the Father?

"And what do you benefit if you gain the whole world but lose your own soul? Is anything worth more than your soul?"
Matthew 16:26 NLT

Discipleship

Scriptures: Luke 6:46, Luke 6:48-49, John 14:15, Matthew 5:48, Micah 6:8, Luke 13:14, John 8:7, John 8:10-11, Luke 9:23-24, Romans 6:6, Matthew 16:26
Additional Scriptures: Galatians 5:24, Acts 20:24

Questions:

1. List where you have lacked obedience to God. Ask God to fill you with the Holy Spirit and commit to confronting the disobedience in your life.

2. What does it mean in your life to "do what is right, to love mercy, and to walk humbly with your God?"

3. What are some aspects of 'self' you need to let go of— pride, greed, desires that increase your status, or something else? Create a plan to crucify your flesh (Galatians 5:24) and explain what that looks like in your life.

Prayer: *Thank You, God for revealing what is pleasing to You. I submit myself to Your Word God and ask that the Holy Spirit reveals and convicts me in those areas where I am disobedient. I acknowledge You, God, as my everything. You are the reason for my existence, You are who I live for my God. Reveal to me, oh Lord, those things of the flesh that I need to crucify. You are my One desire,* *help me to walk in a way pleasing to You. In the powerful name of Jesus, I pray. Amen.*

Day 17:
Living Sacrifice

"And so, dear brothers and sisters, I plead with you to give your bodies to God because of all He has done for you. Let them be a living and holy sacrifice—the kind He will find acceptable. This is truly the way to worship Him."
Romans 12:1 NLT

Obedience means your life is a living sacrifice. Your time is not your own. Your plans, your ministry, your services are all out of your control. However, you can quench the Holy Spirit.

"Do not stop the work of the Holy Spirit."
1 Thessalonians 5:19 ICB

This passage in Thessalonians affirms our capacity to stop the movement of the Holy Spirit. **The movement of God—through the Holy Spirit—will only happen if you allow it.** God gives you the ability to stop the movement of the Holy Spirit. God does not force you to let Him move—you must willingly allow Him.

This means that when ministering, you must be sensitive to the Holy Spirit. There are moments where you must decide what is more important: Is it the Holy Spirit moving, or the schedule you set? Is it God's will or lunch? Is it God or angry people? **Is it GOD?** It should be God. Why has it become so easy to make God the second, third, or last choice?

"Jesus replied, 'You must love the Lord your God with all your heart, all your soul, and all your mind.'"
Matthew 22:37 NLT

How do you love God with all your heart, all you soul, and all your mind? By choosing God first. Our nature contradicts this choice at every moment, but God will honor our commitment by teaching us how to choose His way—every step of our walk of faith.

"Teach me Your way, Lord; I will walk in Your truth; Unite my heart to fear Your name."
Psalm 86:11 NLT

Walking as a living sacrifice requires communication with our Lord God. Even more, it requires that communication to be led by humility—asking for something other than what benefits us or satisfies our flesh, and instead seeking what benefits the Kingdom of God. As disciples, we find that God's Kingdom is not natural to us—it is a foreign concept. But God is more than willing to teach us how to walk in His truth... if we just ask.

"And I will put my Spirit within you, and cause you to walk in my statutes and be careful to obey my rules."
Ezekiel 36:27 ESV

It is God's Spirit within us that leads us to walk the narrow road (Matthew 7:13-14). The Holy Spirit brings conviction when we are in compromising situations. That feeling of conviction reminds us that what we are about to do goes against what God has called us to be. Everyone feels the conviction differently—some describe conviction as a nudge inside, others as a feeling, others remember a scripture that reminds them to choose correctly, some remember a prophetic word spoken to them, and others explain it as a knowing. No matter how the Holy Spirit convicts you, when you are filled with the Holy Spirit, know that He will convict you.

"That is why the Holy Spirit says, Today when you hear His voice, don't harden your hearts as Israel did when they rebelled, when they tested Me in the wilderness."
Hebrews 3:7-8 NLT

The passage in Hebrews is a biblical warning to those who choose to ignore the voice of the Holy Spirit. As we grow in discipleship, the heart of Jesus grows within us. Yet, the daily requirement to die to our flesh can be difficult, especially in areas we are not yet ready to surrender. If we refuse to surrender and continue to ignore the Holy Spirit, our hearts can—and will—become hardened.

"Be careful then, dear brothers and sisters. Make sure that your own hearts are not evil and unbelieving, turning you away from the living God. You must warn each other every day, while it is still 'today,' so that none of you will be deceived by sin and hardened against God."
Hebrews 3:12-13 NLT

Society encourages people to embrace who they are, popularizing "self" as the most important part of every individual. Some ministries fear that confronting "self" will lead to loss of congregants. As a result, Christians are rarely confronted about their own deception in sin. Hardened hearts can sit in the pew next to you every Sunday, having lost the desire to hear God's voice.

The Scripture in Hebrews 3:12-13 places the responsibility of warning other disciples on you. You and I must warn each other daily of the risk that comes with sin in our lives—the risk that leads to hardened hearts that are evil and unbelieving. This type of warning goes against both the desires of our flesh to remain autonomous and the feel-good culture of today's society and the church. Warnings against sin and an ungodly, unbiblical lifestyle are encouragement—even if it is not what someone wants to hear.

The type of obedience required to give these kinds of warnings is difficult in a culture, or ministry, where "encouragement" means only telling people what they want to hear. But obedience, as seen throughout the Word of God, often means saying the things that people don't want to hear. And it must be said, because the responsibility has been given to us by the Lord our God.

"So whether you eat or drink, or whatever you do, do it all for the glory of God."
1 Corinthians 10:31 NLT

Every action, every conversation, every word, every step, every single time you sit at a table to eat or drink, every day at work, every day at home, and every single moment of your life should glorify God. As a disciple, that is the life you are called to live.

Discipleship

Scriptures: Romans 12:1, 1 Thessalonians 5:19, Matthew 22:37, Psalm 86:11, Ezekiel 36:27, Matthew 7:13-14, Hebrews 3:7-8, Hebrews 3:12-13, 1 Corinthians 10:31
Additional Scriptures: Proverbs 27:17

Questions:

1. List areas where you need to choose God first, and reflect on times when you may have stopped the movement of the Holy Spirit.

2. How has the Holy Spirit convicted you? Write about your past convictions or any current ones. Identify how the Holy Spirit communicates with you as you write.

3. Create a plan to implement Hebrews 3:12-13 in your life. Bonus: Do this with an accountability partner.

Prayer: *Lord God, thank You for who You are. You are worthy of everything. Please forgive me for the times I have put myself before You, my God, my King. Thank You for the Helper, the Holy Spirit, I submit to you, convict me God when what I do is against Your will. Help me, Lord, to be the iron that sharpens those around me. Give me the confidence to do Your will. I love You, Lord, and I* *love Your conviction. I bless Your Holy name, in the most precious name, Jesus, I pray. Amen.*

Day 18:
Loving God More Than People

John 12:42-43 NLT
"Many people did believe in him, however, including some of the Jewish leaders. But they wouldn't admit it for fear that the Pharisees would expel them from the synagogue. For they loved human praise more that the praise of God."

As disciples, there is a difference that must be distinguished: the difference between loving people and wanting people to love us. The distinction can make or break the ministry of a disciple—one seeks the will of God, the other seeks the will of people. If you know me, you know one of my favorite sayings is: I refuse to love you to hell.

If you truly love someone, you want the best for them—God's Kingdom. Imagine sitting outside your home on your patio and seeing a toddler alone, wandering towards a busy street. You are going to run out and stop the toddler from going on the street. Going out and making disciples of the nations is no different. Making disciples of nations means stopping those you love from heading towards destruction.

"And you will know the truth, and the truth will set you free."
John 8:32 ESV

Jesus is the freedom people need. Jesus is the freedom that leads to a new life—consecrated, set apart, and free from destruction. As disciples, we are called to share the truth of the gospel. The way to most love someone is by sharing the gospel.

The fear that sharing the gospel will result in people rejecting you or cause you to lose someone's love is a lie from the devil. The rejection of the gospel has nothing to do with you. It is spiritual and has everything to do with the devil. The devil is a liar. The love of God reveals the lies of the enemy through the Holy Spirit, but those revelations come only when we choose God first. If you fear people leaving you more than you fear God, you will never confront the work of the enemy enough to have his schemes revealed to you.

"Those who accept my commandments and obey them are the ones who love me. And because they love me, my Father will love them. And I will love them and reveal myself to each of them."
- Jesus, John 14:21 NLT

Jesus clearly states that those who love Him are the ones who will obey Him and keep His commandments. As disciples, we obey out of love for our Savior Jesus. Obedience is the fruit of our love for Him—a fruit that makes our lives sweeter. God is a good God, who wants good for His disciples. **He responds to our obedience with His revelation.** This truth absolutely amazes me! There is nothing I could ever do to deserve God revealing Himself to me. God, the King of the Universe, Creator of

All, wants to reveal Himself to me because He loves me. And He wants to do the same for you. He loves you that much.

"It is better to take refuge in the Lord than to trust in people."
Psalm 118:8 NLT

Simple, yet one of the most difficult concepts to put into practice. Earthly responsibilities can quickly change the course of our actions when in difficult circumstances. For example, if a disciple decides to go into full-time ministry at a large, thriving church with wealthy members, then putting faith in God may not be very difficult—in fact, faith may not even be required to survive from that ministry. But if you are called to full-time ministry, in a struggling and impoverished community where people may not have funds to survive, then putting your faith in God may be extremely difficult.

This is where Psalm 118:8 becomes essential—if your faith is in God, and you preach His truth, then God will sustain you. Passionate motivational speeches will never break the demonic holds that the gospel of freedom and deliverance will bring. A shortened altar call and an elongated offering message will never bring the revival fire that will draw the crowds for a move of God. **Taking refuge in the Lord means letting God work without relying on the man-made performance we so often fall short in.**

Discipleship

Scriptures: John 12:42-43, John 8:32, John 14:21, Psalm 118:8
Additional Scriptures: Luke 12:49-53, Revelation 12:11, Proverbs 29:25, Ecclesiastes 3:14

Questions:

1. Reflect on a time when you chose a person over God. Create a plan to prioritize God's will over the approval of others, no matter the resistance.

2. Reflect on a time you were disobedient to God. How was the enemy at work in your disobedience?

3. Identify areas where you have relied on people more than God. Submit those areas to God and create a plan to surrender your ministry to Him, noting where reliance on others needs to shift towards dependence on God.

Prayer: *My God, today I choose You. Teach me Your way, Lord as I learn to put You before all. Forgive me, Father, for my times of disobedience. I want to honor You, God, in everything I do. Help my unbelief in the areas of my life where I have not completely relied on You. Holy Spirit, reveal to me the areas where I need to rely on You,* *my God. You are the Almighty God, and I honor You in everything. In the mighty name of Jesus, my Savior, I pray. Amen.*

Day 19:
Loving God More Than the World

1 John 2:15-17 ESV
"Do not love the world or the things in the world. If anyone loves the world, the love of the Father is not in him. For all that is in the world—the desires of the flesh and the desires of the eyes and pride of life—is not from the Father but is from the world. And the world is passing away along with its desires, but whoever does the will of God abides forever."

Everything is spiritual. There is nothing in this world that is outside of God's Kingdom. Every single thing we do must bring glory to God. Every decision you make as you walk through your day either glorifies God—or it does not. We make these choices at every moment.

Take driving in traffic, for an easy example. We all know how quickly the driving skills of others can offend us. Offense shows up anywhere people are involved—at work, in a conversation with friends, or with family. Stress is another trigger—worry can cause us to spiral if we choose to view circumstances in the flesh. Critical moments we normally do not recognize as spiritual, actually are. As disciples, we must work to recognize those pivotal moments.

"You adulterers! Don't you realize that friendship with the world makes you an enemy of God? I say it again: If you want to be a friend of the world, you make yourself an enemy of God."
James 4:4 NLT

The passage in James is clear: what we choose in the world directly correlates with our alignment to Christ. We either choose to align with Him and be a friend of God or align with the world and be God's enemy. It is almost as if we are in the garden at the pivotal moment where Eve exercises her free will. However, as disciples our experience differs significantly because Jesus died for us and resurrected. We have the best advantage because Jesus left us the Helper—the Holy Spirit.

The Holy Spirit is the voice that reminds us how to stand as a friend of God in our pivotal moments—**if we just listen**.

"Seek His will in all you do, and He will show you which path to take."
Proverbs 3:6 NLT

Seek. Disciples seek after God. According to the passage in Proverbs seeking is required to know the path God wants us to take. We cannot hear where we need to go, what we need to choose, or what we need to do without seeking after the face of God. And we cannot just seek Him to hear the answers we want, or to receive something from Him. No. **We must seek Him because He is enough. He is all we need.**

"You will seek me and find me, when you seek me with all your heart."
Jeremiah 29:13 ESV

Seeking God with all our heart is the only way to find Him. He knows our hearts, He knows what seeking Him with all our heart looks like for us. You can't fake it. God is our Creator, He knows where our motives lie and who we really are on the inside. The promise of God is: if you seek Him with all your heart, you will find Him. That is an incredible promise!

"God is not a man, that He should lie, or a son of man, that He should change His mind. Has He said, and will He not do it? Or has He spoken, and will He not fulfill it?"
Numbers 23:19 ESV

It is an incredible promise because it's simple—and true. What God says, He does. God's Word is a roadmap. If we follow it, God promises He will provide all we need to walk according to His Word. **You just need to take that first step of faith and believe His Word enough to see it in action.**

Discipleship

Scriptures: 1 John 2:15-17, James 4:4, Proverbs 3:6,
Jeremiah 29:13, Numbers 23:19
Additional Scriptures: Matthew 22:37, John 5:41-44

Questions:

1. What does it mean to you that every single second of
your day is a part of God's Kingdom? Do you view
mundane task as acts that glorify God? If not, how can you
shift your mindset and heart to view every moment as a
God-moment?

2. Can you recall a pivotal moment this week when you
chose flesh over Godly action?

3. What actions can you take (or implement) to seek God
more intentionally?

Prayer: *Lord God, please help us to recognize when the Holy Spirit
shows us the moments we miss to glorify your name. Bring those
moments to our attention and help us to remember You quickly when
life rapidly spirals into difficulty. God, please shut those doors and
remove those distractions that keep us from being in Your presence
and seeking you. Teach us God to put You first and dwell in Your*

presence, no matter what comes next, teach us to put You first and only You as the priority.

Day 20:
Avoid

1 John 3:8 NLT
"But when people keep on sinning, it shows that they belong to the devil, who has been sinning since the beginning. But the Son of God came to destroy the works of the devil."

Avoid sin. Jesus came to destroy the power of the devil in your life. When you continue to sin after meeting Jesus, it is as if you are picking up the chains that Jesus already broke off of you and wrapping them back around yourself. Even worse, choosing to sin is choosing to negate the power of God through the death and resurrection of our Savior, Jesus Christ. Choosing sin is denying the power and authority of Jesus.

"For people will be lovers of self, lovers of money, boastful, arrogant, slanderers, disobedient to parents, ungrateful, unholy, unloving, irreconcilable, malicious gossips, without self-control, brutal, haters of good, treacherous, reckless, conceited, lovers of pleasure rather than lovers of God, holding to a form of godliness although they have denied its power; avoid such people as these."
2 Timothy 3:2-5 ESV

This list is significant, and we may initially skim through it quickly, failing to recognize where we are represented in this passage of Scripture. But we are represented. As disciples, we should take the time to identify our struggle with sin daily. Second Timothy provides a starting point to recognize what sin looks like in our lives—sin we may not even realize are present in our daily struggles. As disciples, we must identify the flesh struggles and choose to die to those struggles every single day.

"So whoever knows the right thing to do and fails to do it, for him it is sin."
James 4:17 ESV

Sin is choosing to commit an act against the righteousness of God. The deeper you walk with God, the more you realize that everything may not be a *sin issue*, but everything touches the heart of God. **Issues that we do not perceive as sin become questionable. Why? Because when our world revolves around God, we see the world differently.** For example, there are small stressors that others allow to disturb their peace, but God shows us our stresses must be altar moments as disciples. We have to leave all of our struggles at the altar. When we fail to do what is right—even in seemingly small ways—we must ask: is this sin, based on James 4:17?

"No one can serve two masters, for either he will hate the one and love the other, or he will be devoted to the one and despise the other. You cannot serve God and money."
Matthew 6:24 ESV

Money is a motivation—but it cannot be our motivation as disciples. Still, it is often a driving factor of deviation from God's plan. We must depend on God for all our financial needs—not our job, not our ministry, not school, not spouses—only God.

"It would be better if they had never known the way to righteousness than to know it and then reject the command they were given to live a holy life."
2 Peter 2:21 NLT

Lord God, search our hearts! The verse is heavy. The Word of God is telling us that it's better to never have known Jesus—the way to righteousness—than to know Him and reject the command to live a holy life. The grace of God frees us from the chains of the devil. Walking in the grace of God is walking in the freedom He gave us. Free of sin's hold on us—we are no longer slaves to sin. The enemy will make you believe that you can never overcome your sin. But the devil is a liar! **Believing that lie is denying the power of what our Savior, Jesus Christ, accomplished on the cross.**

Discipleship

Scriptures: 1 John 3:8, 2 Timothy 3:2-5, James 4:17, Matthew 6:24, 2 Peter 2:21
Additional Scriptures: Hebrews 6:4-8

Questions:

1. Look up the definitions for each struggle listed in 2 Timothy 3:2-5 (e.g., lovers of self, lovers of money, boastful, arrogant, slanderers, disobedient to parents, ungrateful, unholy, unloving, irreconcilable, malicious gossips, without self-control, brutal, haters of good, treacherous, reckless, conceited, lovers of pleasure rather than lovers of God). Reflect on how and when you have struggled with any of these.

2. Can you identify the sins you are struggling with now? Use the list in 2 Timothy 3:2-5 as a reference to help pinpoint it.

3. Is there something in your life that you never thought of as sin but now realize may grieve the heart of God or hinder your walk with Him? Write it down and ask God for clarity and transformation.

Prayer: *Lord God, thank you for Your power and Your authority given to me by Your Son and my Savior, Jesus Christ. Please forgive me for the times I have struggled with the things You say I should avoid. I confess my sins to You, Lord (confess list from question 2) and I ask that You forgive me and convict me when I place myself in situations that lead to sin and actions that do not glorify You. I want to live for You, my God. Continue to reveal to me those things that I never realized hurt Your heart and Your Kingdom. I thank You, Lord for Your grace over my life. In the name of the One who died for me and rose again, my Savior, Jesus, I pray. Amen.*

Day 21:
Overcoming Temptation

1 John 5:3-5 NLT
"Loving God means keeping His commandments, and His commandments are not burdensome. For every child of God defeats this evil world, and we achieve this victory through our faith. And who can win this battle against the world? Only those who believe that Jesus is the Son of God."

The power of Jesus Christ—what He did for us on the cross and the authority He gave us through His resurrection—is the same power that frees us from sin! As disciples, we cannot sit back and allow the enemy to convince us that we will always deal with our sin habits. The enemy wants to keep you burdened by the sin. The devil wants you to believe that it is just your struggle, it's not! Jesus Christ died for that sin, and He wants to break it off your life. True belief in Jesus means no longer accepting the sin as your struggle and releasing it to Him completely, giving God full control of it. The devil wants you to deny the power of Jesus Christ on the cross. The way the enemy convinces you to deny Jesus is by denying His power over your struggles, including sin.

"Submit yourselves therefore to God. Resist the devil, and he will flee from you."
James 4:7 ESV

When you accept the true authority of Jesus Christ, the devil no longer has power over your life. Your submission to the authority of Jesus is your freedom from the enemy. The Word of God is clear: we must stand in the authority that we have in Jesus Christ and resist the devil. Did you know that another word for resist is combat? That's right, we need to combat the enemy. Remember, there is an ongoing spiritual war around you. As a disciple, you must put on your armor and fight. We are not defeated! Do not allow the devil to defeat you by keeping you bound in darkness. Arise Warrior! Put on your armor and use the Sword of the Spirit to kill your flesh daily!

"And when people escape from the wickedness of the world by knowing our Lord and Savior Jesus Christ and then get tangled up and enslaved by sin again, they are worse off than before. It would be better if they had never known the way to righteousness than to know it and then reject the command they were given to live a holy life. They prove the truth of this proverb: 'A dog returns to its vomit.' And another says, 'A washed pig returns to the mud.'"
2 Peter 2:20-22 NLT

True belief in our Savior, Jesus Christ comes with freedom. But some don't fully receive it—not because they don't want it, but because they can't comprehend it. We may preach the love of Jesus to others and lack confidence in His capacity to love *us* through our sin. Sometimes we struggle with sin because we are too ashamed to bring it to God, we do not want to talk to God about the filthiness we carry and instead we try to hide it from God. The enemy has convinced many that their sin is too great for God to forgive or too small to bother God with—both are lies from the devil! Bring everything to Him.

"And I am certain that God, who began the good work within you, will continue His work until it is finally finished on the day when Christ Jesus returns."
Philippians 1:6 NLT

When Jesus Christ died on the cross, He said "It is finished!" (John 19:30). We must believe that when God does something He does it the right way. As disciples, we are called to strive for the life Jesus Christ died for us to live. Yes, we are complete—perfected in heaven but that's not an excuse to stop striving for holiness here on earth.

As a disciple, how can we believe in the power of God to heal and provide, and not believe in that same power of God to deliver us from our sins? We cannot want the power of God to give us the things that benefit us, like healing and money; and deny the power of God when it comes to the things that please us and not God, like sin.

Is it sad that we can boil down many prayers to healing and money? A new job. New car. New house. We have become so accustomed to praying for what we want that we have completely lost the heart of God. Much of what we ask for revolves around us and then we call it 'kingdom living.' No. True Kingdom living is not about what we can get—it's about what we surrender. It's an upside-down Kingdom.

"For the desire of the flesh is against the Spirit, and the Spirit against the flesh; for these are in opposition to one another, in order to keep you from doing whatever you want."
Galatians 5:17 NASB2020

As disciples, we must lay our flesh at the feet of Jesus daily.

The flesh is what fights our desire to follow Jesus. We are in a constant spiritual battle. The second we put down our armor the enemy is going to attack. While we are in the flesh, we must fight the flesh. As disciples, we can't just give up and say we will never be perfect, that statement allows the enemy to wreak havoc in our lives. It's as if we are giving the devil permission to put the chains back on us. Instead, proclaim the full victory of Jesus Christ! The blood of Jesus broke the chains that kept us in darkness!

Discipleship

Scriptures: 1 John 5:3-5, James 4:7, 2 Peter 2:20-22,
Philippians 1:6, John 19:30, Galatians 5:17
Additional Scriptures: Psalm 119:45, 2 Corinthians 13:11,
2 Corinthians 3:17, Colossians 2:10

Questions:

1. Is there sin you have been too ashamed to bring to
God? Today, God is asking you to release it to Him. Write
it down as a step of surrender.

2. Find a verse that you can recite when facing temptation
from the enemy. Write the full verse down and work to
memorize it so you can use it as a spiritual weapon when
needed.

3. Declare the victory over every sin you've struggled with.
Make a list of those sins and include them in your prayer
today. This act puts the enemy on notice—the devil now
knows you are going to war with him, and you are going in
already victorious through Christ!

Prayer: *Thank You, Father God for Your victory in me. I praise You, Lord because You planned my victory from before I was in my mother's womb. Lord, I lay down all of my sin here at Your feet (list your answers to questions 1 and 2). I fix my eyes on You, Jesus and I claim my victory through the blood You shed for me on the cross. You are worthy of all my time and all my actions, today I give it all to You, my God. I refuse to let the enemy keep me down because I am victorious in You, Jesus! Thank you for the victory. I love you, Jesus and in Your powerful name, I pray. Amen.*

Discipleship Group
Week 3

Additional Scriptures Shared with the Group:

Questions:

1. Have you ever ignored the prompting of the Holy Spirit? What was the result, and what did you learn? When was a time God revealed Himself to you after you obeyed Him?

2. What are some signs that you are relying on people more than God in your ministry or daily life?

3. What does resisting the devil look like practically for you? How do you suit up spiritually each day for battle?

Prayer Points:
- Walk in authority.
- Radical obedience—living as a sacrifice.
- Pursuing holiness.

Day 22:
Fear God

Revelation 14:7 NLT
"'Fear God,' he shouted. 'Give glory to Him. For the time has come when He will sit as judge. Worship Him who made the heavens, the earth, the sea, and all the springs of water.'"

There is no one like our Lord God Almighty. The immensity of His presence is sometimes lost on us because we cannot fathom the complete greatness of who He is. At times, it is necessary to just sit in His presence and recognize who He is. As disciples, we are called to recognize who God is—we know His voice, His heart, we seek after Him. However, society and the modern church can sometimes lose sight of God in everything else. The reverence is lost. A prophet speaks, and people don't know how to react. So few recognize when God is speaking today. The fear is lost. There is no desire to the hear the voice of God.

"Since we have these promises, beloved, let us cleanse ourselves from every defilement of body and spirit, bringing holiness to completion in the fear of God."
2 Corinthians 7:1 ESV

Truly recognizing and knowing who God is will instill a deeper appreciation for Him and what He can do. The passage in Revelation is true—one day, Jesus will sit in judgment of each of us. This walk of faith is not just a matter of life and death; it is eternal—forever. So much is at stake—your soul and the souls of your generations to come. Who you choose to serve and worship is not just a decision you are making in a two-minute prayer at the end of a church service, nor is it a decision sealed by sitting in a church pew each Sunday. This is so much more. Jesus laid down everything—His whole life—for you. All He asks is that we give Him everything in return.

"Not everyone who calls out to me, 'Lord! Lord!' will enter the Kingdom of Heaven. Only those who actually do the will of my Father in heaven will enter. On judgment day many will say to me, 'Lord! Lord! We prophesied in your name and cast out demons in your name and performed many miracles in your name.' But I will reply, 'I never knew you. Get away from me, you who break God's laws.'"
– Jesus, Matthew 7:21-23 NLT

Identify how that passage makes you feel after reading it. That feeling—that is the fear of the Lord. That is the same fear that should rise up in you when the devil tempts you. When facing temptation, it should be the fear of God saying, "*He never knew you,*" that makes you resist the devil. It is the thought of eternal separation from God, the possibility of your name not being written in the Book of the Lamb, that should drive you to submit completely to the authority of God.

"For God did not send his Son into the world to condemn the world, but in order that the world might be saved through him."
John 3:17 ESV

There is no condemnation for those who are in Christs

Jesus (Romans 8:1), so we are not to live condemned. Jesus Christ came to save us from condemnation. This means we should not be afraid to approach God with our mess. Instead, we should fear not approaching God in surrender—because of who He is and what He did for us. Holding onto condemnation and refusing to surrender that which condemns us is denying the power of God. If we deny the power of God, then we do not truly fear Him.

"Just think how much worse the punishment will be for those who have trampled on the Son of God, and have treated the blood of the covenant, which made us holy, as if it were common and unholy, and have insulted and disdained the Holy Spirit who brings God's mercy to us."
Hebrews 10:29 NLT

The way you live reflects whether you truly believe in what Jesus did. He did what we could never do. He took on our filthiness and sin, and purified us with His righteousness when we deserved death. We belong to Him—He purchased us with His blood (1 Peter 1:18-19). He deserves it all, but we must recognize Him as our everything in order to give Him our all.

"'The human heart is the most deceitful of all things, and desperately wicked. Who really knows how bad it is? But I, the Lord, search all hearts and examine secret motives. I give all people their due rewards, according to what their actions deserve.'"
Jeremiah 17:9-10 NLT

As disciples, we can no longer be satisfied with saying "God knows my heart." That statement should instill the fear of God in you because **God does know your heart— it is the most deceitful of all things**. We should never follow our own hearts. We must follow the heart of God.

The enemy has crept into the church and deceived many

into believing in a god who conforms to the heart of his people and never calls them to change. That is a lie from the devil! We have failed to recognize who God is, and that lack of reverence gives us a false sense of salvation. Jesus did not come to die for you, so you could continue to live in the grip of the enemy. God's power is more than we can understand, and He frees us through that power.

"For all of God's promises have been fulfilled in Christ with a resounding 'Yes!' And through Christ, our 'Amen' (which means 'Yes') ascends to God for His glory."
2 Corinthians 1:20 NLT

When God calls us, our answer should be a resounding "Yes!" Your "Yes" is what glorifies God. Jesus Christ empowered us with His authority to say "Yes" when He died on the cross for us. The Holy Spirit equips our "Yes" by guiding us as our Helper in every step.

We say "No" to God out of disobedience. Saying "No" out of fear of failure means you are relying on your flesh, not the Holy Spirit. It also means that you fear your flesh may be too strong to overcome. That is not the fear of the Lord, it is a reflection of unbelief. You must fear God more than failure. Disciples let the devil know that he does not have the power to make you say "No" to God.

The longer we are in the presence of God, the easier it is to recognize Him. Obedience comes through our recognition of who He is to us.

Discipleship

Scriptures: Revelation 14:7, 2 Corinthians 7:1, Matthew 7:21-23, John 3:17, Romans 8:1, Hebrews 10:29, 1 Peter 1:18-19, Jeremiah 17:9-10, 2 Corinthians 1:20
Additional Scriptures: 1 Corinthians 2:14, 1 John 4:18, Isaiah 6:5

Questions:

1. Ask God to search your heart. Where has your heart been deceitful?

2. Where have you told God no?

3. Explain what has kept you from saying Yes to God.

Prayer: *Father God, place a new heart in me Lord. Search my heart for the things that grieve You, Holy Spirit, and remove them from my life. Break my heart for what breaks Yours. Draw me closer to You, God. Pull me back to You, oh God, when I have wandered away from Your desires, God. Thank you for loving me in my sin and sending my Savior, Jesus, to save me and change me. Help my unbelief in the areas I have told You no before, reveal Yourself to me through the confirmation of Your Word, Jesus. In the majestic name of Jesus, I pray. Amen.*

Day 23:
Humbly Seek God

Everything we have discussed up to now is not possible without seeking God. The only way you love someone, the only way you know someone, and the only way you revere, admire, and appreciate someone is by spending time with them. For the rest of this week, we will study how Jesus instructed us, as disciples, to pray and seek our Father God.

"Pray like this: 'Our Beloved Father, dwelling in the heavenly realms, may the glory of your name be the center on which our lives turn.'"
– *Jesus*, Matthew 6:9 TPT

Jesus gave us a format for seeking the Lord—many know it as the Lord's Prayer. This prayer is a foundational structure for how to approach God when we seek Him. It is not a prayer meant to be repeated verbatim, but rather used as a guide to help us understand every aspect of worship our King desires from us.

First, we must recognize how great our God is—above all

the earth and Ruler of all our lives. As we acknowledge Him, we must realize that every part of who we are must bring glory to our Creator. This aspect of our worship can look different for each of us. For some, it's singing a song to the King. For others, it may be sitting in silence, thinking about the mountains God has moved in your life. Maybe it's praying and asking God to open your eyes to His presence every moment of your life. Maybe it's asking Him to help you find the parts of His greatness you have missed in your routines. It doesn't matter how you do it—what matters is that we intentionally glorify God and invite His glory into every area of our lives, as Jesus emphasized.

"God sits above the circle of the earth. The people below seem like grasshoppers to him! He spreads out the heavens like a curtain and makes his tent from them."
Isaiah 40:22 NLT

Everything is coming together now, as we are in the last full week of study. There is a reason God's greatness is emphasized so often throughout Scripture. Jesus taught us that humility is what catches the attention of our Father. It is a humble heart that recognizes the greatness, power, authority, and most importantly, the love of our King that turns His ear to our prayers.

"Though the Lord is great, he cares for the humble, but He keeps his distance from the proud."
Psalm 138:6 NLT

God does not approve of pride. No matter your calling, title, platform, ministry, or influence—nothing makes you better than anyone else. Disciples are the lowest of lows—lowly in spirit. Pride separates us from God; it is pride that caused Satan's fall from heaven (Isaiah 14:13). The moment we begin comparing ourselves to others and thinking we are "more"—more blessed, more anointed, more knowledgeable—we shift our heart posture. When you come to God with expectations the motives for seeking Him become tainted by what you desire and what you think you deserve. God alone will honor His people and reward them based on their actions (Romans 2:6-11). You should not seek honor or reward based on your earthly positions or platforms God has given you. God has placed you there, and God can take it away (Job 1:21).

"And when they cry out, God does not answer because of their pride."
Job 35:12 NLT

Pride stops your prayers from being answered. God will not hear the prayer of the proud because, to Him, they are empty (Job 35:13). Christianity and the Bible are not about you. We have become so self-involved believing God exists to bless us and give us a life full of pleasures. We seek joy in the pleasures of the flesh and when we do not receive those 'blessings,' we think God is punishing us. Or even scarier still, we think if we have all the pleasures of our flesh—money, a nice house, a nice car—we are blessed. Then, we sit and look at all the great stuff we have surrounding us, thinking "look at how much God loves me because I got everything I wanted."

But do you know who entices with glories and pleasures that gratify the flesh?

"'I will give you the glory of these kingdoms and authority over them,' the devil said, 'because they are mine to give to anyone I please. I will give it all to you if you will worship me.'"
– the devil, Luke 4:6-7 NLT

The devil! The devil is a liar! The passage in Luke shows how the devil tempted Jesus in the wilderness, trying to entice our Savior with worldly pleasures. Jesus showed us that the Kingdom of God is worth far more than anything on earth. God does not pursue you or attract you with worldly possessions. In fact, the upside-down Kingdom of God often looks foolish in the world's eyes.

"Instead, God chose things the world considers foolish in order to shame those who think they are wise. And he chose things that are powerless to shame those who are powerful. God chose things despised by the world, things counted as nothing at all, and used them to bring to nothing what the world considers important. As a result, no one can ever boast in the presence of God."
1 Corinthians 1:27-29 NLT

Everything should revolve around God. When we fully submit to Him, it no longer matters what we have, what title we hold, or how much experience we bring. God uses the least of things to bring to nothing what the world deems valuable.

Discipleship

Scriptures: Matthew 6:9, Isaiah 40:22, Psalm 138:6, Isaiah 14:13, Romans 2:6-11, Job 1:21, Job 35:12, Luke 4:6-7, 1 Corinthians 1:27-29
Additional Scriptures: Psalm 116:1-2, James 4:6, Romans 12:16, Isaiah 2:12, James 1:9-10, Ephesians 4:2, Philippians 2:3, Psalm 82:3, Proverbs 11:2, Jeremiah 23:24, Psalm 121:1-2

Questions:

1. Reflect on how much time you have spent in the presence of God. Create a plan to spend more intentional time in His presence.

2. How do you glorify and lift up the name of Almighty God when you are in His presence?

3. Identify areas in your prayers where pride may have influenced your request to God.

Prayer: *Lord God, I humbly come before glorifying Your name. Thank You for allowing me in Your presence. Here in Your presence is where I want to be, Jesus. I commit to You today, God, I will devote more of my time to You, my God. Holy Spirit show me the areas of my life where pride needs to be removed, I submit these areas* *to You (list answers to question 3). In the name of my King, Jesus, I pray. Amen.*

Day 24:
Kingdom Come

Matthew 6:10 TPT
*"Manifest your kingdom realm, and cause your every purpose to be
fulfilled on earth, just as it is in heaven."*

There has been overwhelming discussion on what it means
to let God lead your life as a disciple. But you cannot live a
life led by God without being in constant communication
with Him. And there is no one more capable of directing
you into His will than God Himself.

The free will God gives us allows us to follow whatever we
choose. Still, He desires that we choose Him. God longs to
lead us in our everyday lives so that we can reach the
purpose He has created us for. So logically, our prayer
should include us asking God for His will and purpose to
be fulfilled in our lives—here on earth, just as in heaven.

*"God has no use for the prayers of the people who won't listen to
Him."*
Proverbs 28:9 MSG

The moment Christianity starts revolving around you, it becomes religion. Religion is a set of routines, traditions, and rituals that people follow to meet the criteria required for a certain spiritual belief. Discipleship is not that—it's a relationship. Being a follower of Jesus isn't about just attending church every Sunday, nor is it about expecting God to fulfill your every desire. I want this to be clear: it's not about you.

In a kingdom, the authority ultimately rests with the King. A hierarchical system those lower in rank do not dictate the will of the King—yet, we often live as if we do. We refuse to submit completely to the King, then expect Him to listen, respond, and comply with our every whim, presuming we know best. We do not. Scripture like Proverbs 28:9 warns us: if we reject God's Word and His instruction, He will not respond to our prayers.

If that's hard to hear, it's because it's meant to stir us. When we assume God has blessed certain areas of our lives while we live in disobedience, we need to examine our hearts. Thank God for His Word, which brings clarity, correction, and revelation to our lives. God warns us in Hosea 4:6: if we create our own religion because we have not studied God's Word, we will be destroyed.

"The Lord is far from the wicked, but He hears the prayers of the righteous."
Proverbs 15:29 NLT

The activation of God's will in your life is what opens the door to His promises. God is so merciful because He gives us the answer. His Word teaches us how allowing Him to have full control will impact our lives. He teaches us how without Him, we create chaos. He shows us how disobedience and allowing the enemy access to who we are hinder our communication with Him. The kindness of

God is so great because He gives us the instructions to living in victory. And that path is always through Him.

"Search me, O God, and know my heart; test me and know my anxious thoughts. Point out anything in me that offends you, and lead me along the path of everlasting life."
Psalm 139:23-24 NLT

This is my favorite prayer and one of the most powerful prayers you can pray. When we ask for God's will to be done, we must also be willing to let Him reveal what is standing in the way. What's in our heart, our thoughts, or our habits that offends God and what blocks His will from flowing freely in our lives?

The grace of God is astonishing. He desires to purify us, and He invites us to ask Him for that purification. The gospel is about freedom from bondage—the breaking of every chain the enemy has placed on us. Jesus came to this world to destroy every hold the enemy had on us, including death. If God can do *that*, He is surely pleased when we come to Him with a desire to be refined and transformed. Disciples should have the heart posture expressed in Psalm 139:23-24—a desire to please the Lord God Almighty.

Discipleship

Scriptures: Matthew 6:10, Proverbs 28:9, Hosea 4:6,
Proverbs 15:29, Psalm 139:23-24
Additional Scriptures: Psalm 51:10, James 4:8, Isaiah
1:16, Psalm 66:10

Questions:

1. Identify times where you presented a request to the
King of Kings without considering whether the request
aligned with the Kingdom of Heaven.

2. Reflect on areas where the motions of "Christianity"
became religious in your life rather than flowing from your
relationship with Jesus.

3. Pray Psalm 139:23-24 and write down anything the Lord
reveals that may be offending Him or keeping you from
His will.

Prayer: *My God, let me bless you by being who you want me to be,
take out all that is against Your will and Your heart, God. Convict
me, Lord, when my discipleship becomes religious, I want a
relationship with You, my Savior. Purify me and lead me down the
path of righteousness, Jesus. Help me to rid my life of those things*

You find offensive in me (list answers to question 3). I live to glorify Your name, Jesus, in Your mighty name I pray. Amen.

Day 25:
Daily Bread

Matthew 6:9 TPT
"We acknowledge you as our Provider of all we need each day."

As disciples, our dependance and reliance are in God. He will always give us what we need. He wants to satisfy our needs—He is the One who will complete us. Before we discuss how God fulfills our every need, we need to take a moment to realize that God knows us better than anyone else.

"O Lord, you have examined my heart and know everything about me. You know when I sit down or stand up. You know my thoughts even when I'm far away. You see me when I travel and when I rest at home. You know everything I do. You know what I am going to say even before I say it, Lord."
Psalm 139:1-4 NLT

God, in His abundant grace, gives us the assurances we need throughout His Word. He reassures us by making sure we understand that He knows us. The fact that He knows us gives us the confidence to trust that He loves us and He cares about us.

It's difficult to trust someone you do not know. In the same manner, it's just as challenging to trust someone with the livelihood of you and your family if you don't believe that person understands your needs. The Word of God provides countless scriptures to alleviate the fear of not knowing God—or thinking He doesn't know you. Having the Creator as your Provider is a beautiful relationship. Who better to provide for you than the One who created you?

"So don't worry about these things, saying, 'What will we eat? What will we drink? What will we wear?' These things dominate the thoughts of unbelievers, but your heavenly Father already knows all your needs. Seek the Kingdom of God above all else, and live righteously, and he will give you everything you need."
– Jesus, Matthew 6:31-33 NLT

Jesus reassures us by helping us comprehend the depth of His care for us. He takes those things that most concern us and instructs that those are the concerns that dominate the thoughts of unbelievers. Well, that is convicting—Jesus help us.

As disciples, we must ask: why are our thoughts the same as thoughts of unbelievers? This is where we return to the cornerstone of the gospel—John 3:16—with its key message: belief is what differentiates a disciple from an unbeliever. It is your belief, your faith, that activates the disciple within.

If you truly believe in John 3:16, then you are a believer. Now is the time to confront all the traditions, assumptions, and half-teachings you have established in your walk of faith. It's time to fully accept the gospel and believe in Jesus.

If your thoughts are dominated by the same concerns as unbelievers… if your prayers revolve around yourself and not God's will… if the fruits of your life are not those of a believer… if you have put people and possessions before God… if your faith in God takes second place to your job or your own ability to provide—then praise God for His mercy! God is bringing instruction and clarity where there was once confusion. **Now, is the time to activate your belief in Jesus Christ, our Savior and awaken the disciple within you!**

"So if you sinful people know how to give good gifts to your children, how much more will your heavenly Father give good gifts to those who ask him."
-Jesus, Matthew 7:11 NLT

Jesus simply instructs us to bring our needs—both physically and spiritually—to God and have faith that God will provide. Remember, God knows you. He knows what you need, and He will always keep His promises. That is why it's important to ask according to God's will.

Our daily bread is what we need to survive. Food is a physical need, but even more importantly, the Bread of Life is our spiritual need.

"Jesus replied, 'I am the bread of life. Whoever comes to me will never be hungry again. Whoever believes in me will never be thirsty.'"
John 6:35 NLT

You see, with Jesus we have all we need. He is our everything. **In Him we are complete.** All we have to do is believe it and live a life that reflects our faith in Him. If we live like that, it does not matter what happens around you, His promise is always going to come to pass. Awaken, O disciple! Now is the time to live like a believer!

Discipleship

Scriptures: Matthew 6:9, Psalm 139:1-4, Matthew 6:31-33, John 3:16, Matthew 7:11, John 6:35
Additional Scriptures: Jeremiah 1:5, Psalm 139, John 10:14-15, Matthew 10:30, 1 Corinthians 8:3, Matthew 6:26, Psalm 23:1

Questions:

1. Have you struggled recognizing God as your Provider?

2. What does "The Lord is my shepherd; I have all that I need." (Psalm 23:1 NLT) mean to you?

3. What does true belief look like in your life? Is it different from before today's reading?

Prayer: *Lord God, thank you for your mercy. Thank you for your provision, Father. I surrender all of my desires and wants to you, take them and exchange them for what you want in my life. My God, please give me what I need to fulfill your purpose for me. Give me Jesus and the presence of Your Holy Spirit daily. I trust you and I give you, my heart. In the merciful name of Jesus, Amen.*

Day 26:
Forgiveness

Matthew 6:12 ICB
"Forgive the sins we have done, just as we have forgiven those who did wrong to us."

Jesus took the beating at the time of His death on the cross to save every single person who was trying to kill Him. Jesus would have let any one of those Romans, who killed Him do it all over again if it meant reconciling them to the Father. That is the example of forgiveness that Jesus gives us.

Many have been taught to forgive in a manner contrary to the Word of God. When Jesus reconciled us to the Father through His forgiveness, He did not place any boundaries between us and Himself because of our past. In the same way, we shouldn't place boundaries when we forgive others.

"Instead, be kind to each other, tenderhearted, forgiving one another, just as God through Christ has forgiven you."
Ephesians 4:32 NLT

The way we interact with others is often based on our feelings. But our feelings are fickle, and our heart is deceiving. The feelings we have should be shaped by what God desires for us, not the hurt that makes you withhold forgiveness or place boundaries.

"Then Peter came to him and asked, 'Lord, how often should I forgive someone who sins against me? Seven times?' 'No, not seven times,' Jesus replied, 'but seventy times seven!'"
Matthew 18:21-22 NLT

If Jesus wanted us to forgive the way the world teaches us to, there would be no reason to ever forgive someone seventy times seven. We would have set boundaries so quickly, it would be a miracle if we allowed ourselves to be hurt seven times. And the way Peter asked the question suggests he was thinking the same thing—seven times already seemed like too many.

"'If you forgive those who sin against you, your heavenly Father will forgive you. But if you refuse to forgive others, your Father will not forgive your sins.'"
Matthew 6:14-15 NLT

It is the forgiveness of Jesus that shows us what true forgiveness looks like. No words can express how grateful I am for the way Jesus reconciled us to our Father, God. The Word of God tells us again and again to forgive in the same way we were forgiven.

After everything we've studied—just in the verses within this book—we can say with confidence that, after forgiving our sin, God did not place a boundary between us and Him. In fact, the death of Jesus was the ultimate sacrifice to remove any boundary that sin created. Forgiveness was meant to close the gap between us and

God. That is also how forgiveness should work with those who hurt us.

Why? Because, as disciples, everything we do should glorify God. The incomprehensible love God has for us is most evident in His forgiveness of our sins. What better way to win a soul for Christ than by offering what the world rarely offers—true forgiveness?

Jesus gave us the perfect example of how to treat those who are against us:

"Then Simon Peter drew a sword and slashed off the right ear of Malchus, the high priest's slave. But Jesus said to Peter, 'Put your sword back into its sheath. Shall I not drink from the cup of suffering the Father has given me?'"
John 18:10-11 NLT
"But Jesus said, 'No more of this.' And he touched the man's ear and healed him."
Luke 22:51 NLT

Simon Peter reacted in anger when Judas betrayed Jesus, and in that anger, Simon Peter cut off the ear of one who came to arrest Jesus. But Jesus—who was the one being arrested—rebuked Peter, ordering him to stop and put away the sword. ***Then*, Jesus healed the ear of the person arresting him!**

Peter reacted the way any of us would when someone innocent is about to be harmed. But Jesus showed us another way of confronting evil.

"If your enemy is hungry, feed him. If he is thirsty, give him a drink. Doing this will be like pouring burning coals on his head. And the Lord will reward you."
Proverbs 25:21-22 ICB

Jesus teaches us that when we react in a way that contradicts the world, people will see Jesus in us. No one, apart from our Lord God, would react the way Jesus did in that moment.

I know we are all thinking: *how?* How could we ever react like Jesus? Don't worry. Remember, God knows what we need. God knows forgiveness is not easy. That's one reason why He sent the Holy Spirit—our Helper. These difficult tasks are the perfect times to create that conversation with God. That is what God is waiting for. He longs to be in a relationship with you, and the Holy Spirit desires to lead and teach you.

"If I had not confessed the sin in my heart, the Lord would not have listened."
Psalm 66:18 NLT

Now that we've gone through the process of forgiving others, we know that God will forgive us, just as He promises in the passage above from Matthew 6:14-15. But here, God gives us another heart posture check: He will not listen to our prayers without us confessing the sins in our heart. Confession is an act that requires humility.

The favor of God is so great because His instructions require humility in every act. And by the time a disciple reaches this point in the journey, humility begins to feel natural. That is where we always want to be as disciples—living in humility.

Discipleship

Scriptures: Matthew 6:12, Ephesians 4:32, Matthew 18:21-22, Matthew 6:14-15, John 18:10-11, Luke 22:51, Proverbs 25:21-22, Psalm 66:18
Additional Scriptures: Isaiah 1:15

Questions:

1. Spend as much time as you need to forgive, do not leave this section until you really feel like you are in a much better place of forgiveness towards those who have hurt you the most. It is a process, it may not all be done today, but we do not want to deny the power of the Holy Spirit to help us get to where we need to be.

2. Reflect on those times you have let your feelings control your reactions. Create a plan that allows God control your reactions and implements a Godly view of hurtful situations.

3. What does reconciliation with those who require your forgiveness look like? What does truly loving your enemies look like in your life?

Prayer: *Jesus, You showed me the perfect example of love and forgiveness. Lord, You know how hard it can be to forgive those who* have hurt me. Lord, You also know all that I have been through in life, sometimes it feels like the world is against me. Help me to see Your creation in every single person. Help me to love them, as You have loved me. Help me to see the lost, even when their actions hurt me. Renew my broken heart and heal the hurts, so that I can share Your healing with others, no matter what they have done. I am so undeserving of all You did for me, still, You came to this world, You died, and You resurrected so that I could be with You in eternity. I live in gratitude to You, Jesus. I choose to live that gratitude by sharing the gospel to all, even those who I struggle to forgive. I forgive them, Lord, just as You forgive me. In the name of my Savior, Jesus Christ, I pray. Amen.

Day 27:
Lead Us Not into Temptation

Matthew 6:13 ESV
"And lead us not into temptation, but deliver us from evil."

Last week, we discussed the emphasis the Word of God places on overcoming temptation. Still, the focus of Jesus in this prayer is different—and key to following the will of God. **Jesus is trying to tell us that where we are matters.**

The moment we accept Jesus, some of us begin to underestimate the devil. But the devil has been doing this for thousands of years—he knows exactly how your mind works. He has studied how to destroy your purpose in God since the day you were born. Not only that, but the devil knows your weak spots.

In times of war, countries study their enemy to identify the weak points to attack. What makes you think the devil is any different? There are demons assigned to fight for your soul from birth. The devil knows exactly what situation to put you in to tempt you into sin. The devil knows what music you listened to when you used to drink. The devil knows what friends you were with when you went out clubbing or gambling. The devil knows the people you are unwilling to forgive. The devil knows what makes you angry. The devil knows how to make someone fall into lust. The devil knows what time you have to be at work and what part of the highway you need to get cut off on to lose your temper.

The devil knows all of this, yet we act like he doesn't. We refuse to study the Word of God, and we refuse to acknowledge that we are in the middle of a spiritual war zone. **Angel armies and demons are warring over every soul—including yours! This is life or death.**

"And give no opportunity to the devil."
Ephesians 4:27 ESV

This prayer is Jesus telling us: we cannot give an opportunity to the devil. We are called to be set apart and sanctified for a reason. When you place yourself in a situation that you know will lead to temptation, it's like walking into the devil's living room and saying, "I'm here to play with fire." Nothing in your spiritual walk should be left to chance. This is not a game—it's your soul. And not just your soul, but the souls of your generations to come. Your family, your friends, and those that God has appointed to cross paths with you, all depend on your decision to go all in with God.

"Don't do as the wicked do, and don't follow the path of evildoers. Don't even think about it; don't go that way. Turn away and keep moving."
Proverbs 4:14-15 NLT

As a disciple, this is how we should live our life. We can no longer compromise. We can no longer sit silently in rooms with people and approve of their sin. God did not call us to do that. God called us to walk into the room with Jesus. Our Great Commission is to make disciples of the nations, not to blend in with the nations.

There is absolutely no way we can apply everything that we've learned over the last four weeks if we are deliberately placing ourselves in the hands of the tempter. When we do that, we take away God's authority in our lives and give it to the devil—that is **not** the life of a disciple.

"So now we can tell who are children of God and who are children of the devil. Anyone who does not live righteously and does not love other believers does not belong to God."
1 John 3:10 NLT

How you live matters. What you do matters. Where you go matters. God's Word is clear: **if you do not live righteously, you are not God's child.** Please understand—it's not me saying this—it's the Word of God. My fear is that if I don't write this plainly and you don't read your Bible, you will perish because you refuse to learn. God has been so merciful, giving us every opportunity and tool to follow His will.

"Then he said, 'You son of the devil, full of every sort of deceit and fraud, and enemy of all that is good! Will you never stop perverting the true ways of the Lord?'"
Acts 13:10 NLT

As disciples, we are called to bring an end to the perversion in the Church. The day of the Lord's return is coming, and after everything we've read in Scripture, we must ask: Are we truly willing to follow Jesus? If so, then it's time to turn your life around and sound the alarm for others. Discipleship is costly—and for some, it's an unexpected lifestyle. But every Scripture God gives us is a tool to do discipleship His way.

"The temptations in your life are no different from what others experience. And God is faithful. He will not allow the temptation to be more than you can stand. When you are tempted, he will show you a way out so that you can endure."
1 Corinthians 10:13 NLT

In this passage God reassures you that no matter what the devil throws at you, you can overcome it. There is no temptation that is too much for you. But Jesus also knows our flesh is weak.

"Keep watch and pray, so that you will not give in to temptation. For the spirit is willing, but the body is weak!"'
-Jesus, Matthew 26:41 NLT

Disciples are always on watch. We know the Lord's return is near, and we are called to expand the Kingdom of God. We also know the devil sees our victory in Christ Jesus— and that's what fuels the demonic spiritual warfare against us. But we must arise as disciple warriors against the kingdom of darkness.

Jesus graciously warns us that we must consistently pray and ask God to lead us in His direction. The Holy Spirit's conviction is the voice deep within that alerts us when it's time to remove ourselves from temptation. As disciples, God is giving us the answer: ask for God's direction and He will provide a way out of temptation. When we spend time in the presence of God, we allow the Holy Spirit to strengthen us. Throughout Scripture, Jesus reveals how important time in His presence is.

Discipleship

Scriptures: Matthew 6:13, Ephesians 4:27, Proverbs 4:14-15, 1 John 3:10, Acts 13:10, 1 Corinthians 10:13, Matthew 26:41

Additional Scriptures: James 1:13, Hebrews 4:15, 2 Timothy 4:18, Isaiah 43:2

Questions:

1. Identify your weak spots. What situations should you avoid that tempt you to sin?

2. Create a plan to truly follow God's Word. What changes do you need to make to live as a child of God?

3. Identify specific times when you've heard the Word of the Lord taught deceitfully. Where have you seen God's truth perverted (e.g. social media, sermons, books)?

Prayer: *Thank You, God, for Your revelation. You have revived me through Your revelation, continue to reveal to me, Lord, the weak areas where I have given access to the devil. Holy Spirit, open my eyes to the things that pervert the Word you have given me. Help me to recognize when deceit is taught, I want to know Your voice so well, God, that I can discern the contradictions. You are so good, God. You are gracious in Your instruction and I long to know You in a* *way that will keep me walking in down Your righteous path, Almighty and Wonderful God. In the glorious name of Jesus, I pray. Amen.*

Day 28:
The Oil

Matthew 25:10-12 NLT

"But while they were gone to buy oil, the bridegroom came. Then those who were ready went in with him to the marriage feast, and the door was locked. Later, when the other five bridesmaids returned, they stood outside, calling, 'Lord! Lord! Open the door for us!' But he called back, 'Believe me, I don't know you!'"

In the parable of the ten brides, five of the brides were foolish and ran out of oil. The other five "wise" brides did not let any of the foolish brides borrow their oil. In the same way, you cannot borrow the anointing.

"'Command the people of Israel to bring you pure oil of pressed olives for the light, to keep the lamps burning continually. The lampstand will stand in the Tabernacle, in front of the inner curtain that shields the Ark of the Covenant. Aaron and his sons must keep the lamps burning in the Lord's presence all night. This is a permanent law for the people of Israel, and it must be observed from generation to generation.'"
Exodus 27:20-21 NLT

We need to be pressing for our oil. The parable of the ten brides is similar to this scripture in Exodus, where the people of Israel were commanded to press olives for the oil that would light the lamp in the Tabernacle continually. Aaron and his sons were tasked to keep the lamps burning in the Lord's presence all night, just as the brides from the parable in Matthew.

When ministering to the Lord—even if it's done in front of people—it must still be done unto the Lord. As disciples, we must press for oil daily and then pour it out onto the feet of Jesus when we minister. We press by spending time in the presence of our God. Prayer is a requirement for a disciple. Ministry is a sacred moment between you and the Lord—but the anointing only comes through the pressing. After the pressing, we break that jar of oil at His feet. He is always our audience of One—our King, Jesus.

As disciples, we do not borrow from someone else's oil. We do not wait for someone to pour into us and then take their oil and use it. No, as disciples, we present ourselves unto the Lord as an offering—pleasing and acceptable to God. We press for the oil from Him alone.

"Work hard so you can present yourself to God and receive his approval. Be a good worker, one who does not need to be ashamed and who correctly explains the word of truth."
2 Timothy 2:15 NLT

For example, I am not against reading books— obviously—but my oil cannot come from a book that someone else has written. That would be borrowing oil from someone else. My oil must come from the King of Kings. The oil comes from my time spent with Him, from reading His Word, from my time in prayer. It comes from the pressing.

If you are ministering unto the Lord God before His people, then you must collect your anointing oil **before** you minister. Otherwise, it is just words—and it is NOT anointed.

I have experienced situation where I've asked the Lord "God, what do I do?" And I distinctly hear His answer: "Do not let them take your oil. It needs to be poured out to ME. You pressed it for ME."

The oil helps you discern:

"I write these things to you about those who are trying to deceive you. But the anointing that you received from Him abides in you, and you have no need that anyone should teach you. But as His anointing teaches you about everything, and is true, and is no lie—just as it has taught you, abide in Him."
1 John 2:26-27 ESV

The oil comes from loving righteousness—the truly holy things:

"You have loved righteousness and hated wickedness. Therefore God, your God, has anointed you with the oil of gladness beyond your companions."
Psalm 45:7 ESV

The oil brings favor:

"You prepare a feast for me in the presence of my enemies. You honor me by anointing my head with oil. My cup overflows with blessings."
Psalm 23:5 NLT

It's time to return to ministering unto the Lord—to be the bride who waits only for Him, pressing into the only thing we need: our Savior.

Discipleship

Scriptures: Matthew 25:10-12, Exodus 27:20-21, 2 Timothy 2:15, 1 John 2:26-27, Psalm 45:7, Psalm 23:5
Additional Scriptures: Luke 7:38, Joel 2:28-29

Questions:

1. Have you borrowed from the oil of someone else?

2. Create a plan to press for your oil. Consider your daily schedule, how you press into God's presence, and your past experiences in God's presence.

3. Reflect on a time you ministered from an empty jar of oil. What challenges did you face ministering without having been in God's presence?

Prayer: *Lord God, thank You for keeping me in Your presence. I long to be in Your presence more, God. Forgive me, for the times I have tried to do this without You Lord Jesus. Today, I recognize that I cannot pour into others without You, God. I don't want to do this without You, I want You to lead me, Lord. Holy Spirit convict me when I move forward without You. Thank you, God, for loving me to revelation of Your heart. I once again, commit to Your leading. In Your gracious name, I pray, Jesus. Amen*

Discipleship Group
Week 4

Additional Scriptures Shared with the Group:

Questions:

1. Examine the different ways in which compromises have impacted the Christian culture and the church. Determine the steps that a disciple should take in their daily life in response to these compromises.

2. Evaluate common assumptions that are widely acknowledged but may not align with biblical teachings.

3. Discuss how your value of the Bible has changed throughout this study.

Prayer Points:
- Activation of the Holy Spirit.
- Commissioning the disciple within.
- Courage to confront compromise.

Day 29:
The Upside-Down Kingdom

Jeremiah 29:11 NLT
"For I know the plans I have for you,' says the Lord. They are plans for good and not for disaster, to give you a future and a hope."'

People often say that God wants us to live our best life here on earth—heaven on earth. But sometimes, people apply this idea using the world's definition of what "best" means, and that is a misapplication. We have no true standards, we don't actually know what is best for us. God has the standard. God knows what is best for us. So, when God says He has plans for us—plans to prosper us—that does not automatically mean prosperity the way the world defines it.

"'Don't store up treasures here on earth, where moths eat them and rust destroys them, and where thieves break in and steal. Store your treasures in heaven, where moths and rust cannot destroy, and thieves do not break in and steal. Wherever your treasure is, there the desires of your heart will also be."'
Matthew 6:19-21 NLT

Many people desire to prosper in ways that reflect prosperity in a first-world country like the United States. However, the Word of God applies to the entire world—not just one country. There are countless brothers and sisters in Christ around the globe who cannot experience prosperity in that way, yet they are still prospering in Christ—because He is all they need. **For some reason, in the western world, we often find ourselves unsatisfied if God doesn't give us everything we want.** But our desires should align with His true desires. God's Kingdom is upside down. You can't turn it into a kingdom that exists to serve your pleasures and still call it God's.

"For the world offers only a craving for physical pleasure, a craving for everything we see, and pride in our achievements and possessions. These are not from the Father, but are from this world."
1 John 2:16 NLT

What are your desires? What are you chasing in life? What are your goals and aspirations? Are your goals centered around you—or around God? As disciples, we can use the passage in 1 John to evaluate the posture of our hearts. Discipleship is a lifestyle, and evaluating our hearts and thoughts should be a daily process. As God leads and directs us, all we need to do is obey. This study includes a significant amount of Scripture to show that discipleship cannot be based on a surface-level application of a few verses heard once a week at church. The Word of God overflows with instruction, direction, and wisdom for how to live a life that pleases our Father, Almighty God.

"By his divine power, God has given us everything we need for living a godly life. We have received all of this by coming to know Him, the One who called us to Himself by means of His marvelous glory and excellence."
2 Peter 1:3 NLT

Honestly, I'm not sure when confusion crept in or how we ended up with such a compromised Church. But God is calling His disciples to arise and stand for truth. He's calling you. He's calling me. Are you ready to answer that call? God has already given us everything we need to walk in His purpose and war for His Kingdom. Please do not miss what God has been showing you. His Word is a cup that overflows with His love for you. If you are not reading it, you're hurting yourself. God gave it all—for you. Now is the time to truly believe. If you're reading this, it means that God cares deeply for you and is calling you to go deeper.

"Jesus entered the Temple and began to drive out all the people buying and selling animals for sacrifice. He knocked over the tables of the money changers and the chairs of those selling doves. He said to them, 'The Scriptures declare, 'My Temple will be called a house of prayer,' but you have turned it into a den of thieves!'"
Matthew 21:12-13 NLT

Just as Jesus flipped the tables of compromise in the Temple, He is calling us to flip the tables of compromise in our own lives—and in the Church! Take the step of faith. Flip your life upside-down. Find your true identity in Christ—not in who you were or what you've done.

"We know that our old life died with Christ on the cross. This was so that our sinful selves would have no power over us, and we would not be slaves to sin."
Romans 6:6 ICB

Lose your old self. Seek God until you find Him—and you will find Him (Jeremiah 29:13). This is God's radical call to you: the time has come to shake the earth, because His return is near. Consecrate yourself. Return to your first love—the One who knew you before you were formed.

Arise, O Warrior! The time has come to step onto the battlefield of compromise and gain territory for our Almighty God!

Discipleship

Scriptures: Jeremiah 29:11, Matthew 6:19-21, 1 John 2:16,
2 Peter 1:3, Matthew 21:12-13, Romans 6:6, Jeremiah 29:13
Additional Scriptures: Proverbs 30:7-9, 2 Timothy 4:2,
Matthew 19:21, Matthew 20:16, John 15:8

Questions:

1. Identify areas where you expected God to fulfill your
worldly desires. Reflect on how to apply the Kingdom of
God to those desires and reshape them into godly desires.

2. Identify new instruction, direction, or wisdom you've
received from God this past month. Create a plan to
implement it into your daily life.

3. Identify tables of compromise you need to flip in your
own life.

Prayer: *My God, thank you for loving me enough to bring
correction to my life. Please forgive me for those times when I confused
Your Kingdom with the desires of the world. Forgive me for those
times I placed my faith in the world and not in Your Kingdom, God.
Flip the tables of compromise in my life, Jesus. Show me Your heart,
God. Give me confidence in Your authority, Jesus, to enter the*

battlefield of compromise and confront the deceit of the enemy. Today, I am stepping into my new life in You, Jesus. The devil no longer has authority over me, the days of compromise our gone with my old self. I declare I am new in You, Jesus. In Your Powerful name, Jesus, I pray. Amen.

Day 30:
Awakened by the Word

Law School taught me one of the most valuable lessons of my life: people cannot value what they do not understand. Let me explain.

There is value in a law degree—you learn to write professionally, search for inconsistencies, and identify mistruths. You learn that to truly know something, you must identify each fact, know it, memorize it, and be ready to defend it. You gain skills in analysis, professional presentation, public speaking, and you open doors to connections that were previously unavailable.

However, everyone in your daily life who did not attend law school has no idea of your capabilities. Assumptions are made, such as: if you went to law school, you should work in court, start a law firm, or take legal cases. But those assumptions are based on the misunderstanding that a law degree only holds value in a courtroom.

In Christianity, people act in much the same way. There is a lack of realization regarding the value of the Word of

God. That inability to recognize its value leads to a Bible left unread. Instead, many function based on their own assumptions of God's Word—a dangerous place to be as a "Christian." The faith walk with God is never fully realized because the value is never understood.

"All Scripture is inspired by God and is useful to teach us what is true and to make us realize what is wrong in our lives. It corrects us when we are wrong and teaches us to do what is right. God uses it to prepare and equip His people to do every good work."
2 Timothy 3:16-17 NLT

When you read the Bible, the Holy Spirit brings understanding. Wisdom is gained, knowledge grows, and all of a sudden, your walk with God changes—because commitment to His Word has led to a newfound value. The more you read, the more you realize that God gave you His Word to live out a life in Him—where joy is not dependent on your circumstances or possessions, but on His presence.

"Your word is a lamp to my feet and a light to my path."
Psalm 119:105 ESV

God is generous in His grace. Not everything in life comes with instructions, but discipleship does. There is no reason to ignore everything God has given us. In fact, when we do ignore it, life becomes more complicated. Once you decide to submit to God and walk in that submission, you begin to see life differently—and your priorities change. Life just gets better.

"But don't just listen to God's word. You must do what it says. Otherwise, you are only fooling yourselves."
James 1:22 NLT

We have been fools for far too long! God, out of His love

for us, has brought revelation and prepared us to take a stand for His Kingdom. We are now equipped and ready to answer the call to discipleship!

Discipleship

Scriptures: 2 Timothy 3:16-17, Psalm 119:105, James 1:22
Additional Scriptures: Isaiah 6:8, Psalm 78

Questions:

1. Have you undervalued the Bible? Create a plan to increase your time in God's Word.

2. Have you ever made an assumption about the ways of the Lord without verifying that it truly aligns with the Word of God? For example, a common saying is, "God will not give you more than you can handle." But yes—He does! In our weakness, He shows up in perfect power (2 Corinthians 12:9). God handles what we cannot, but He gives it to us so that we learn to be obedient and submit everything to Him.

3. Identify any fears that keep you from fully submitting to God. Lay them at God's feet today.

Prayer: *Father, what a mighty God You are! Forgive me, Lord, for failing to recognize the value of Your instruction, direction, and wisdom—Your Word. Today, I commit to spending more time in scripture to learn to recognize Your voice. Please forgive me when I have made assumptions contrary to who You truly are God. I give* *you all of my fears today, (list your answer to question 3). I choose to walk in Your freedom, truly following Your Word. Here I am, God, send me as Your disciple. In the majestic name of Jesus, my Savior, I pray. Amen.*

Discipleship Group
Week 5

Additional Scriptures Shared with the Group:

Questions:

1. How has your understanding of "prosperity" changed after reflecting on the upside-down values of God's Kingdom?

2. What does it mean to "flip the tables of compromise" in your own life? What tables still need to be overturned?

3. Why do you think people in today's culture—including Christians—often undervalue Scripture?

4. Now that you've finished the 30-day journey, how will you walk differently as a disciple going forward?

Prayer Points:
- Renewed minds to value God's Word.
- Opened eyes to compromised Christianity.
- Awaken the disciple within.

Notes:

Notes:

Notes: